An Old Texan's Poetry

Roy Jackson

Printed in the United States of America.

Library of Congress Control Number: 2020910680

ISBN   Paperback   978-1-64803-768-9
              Hardback   978-1-64803-769-6
              eBook   978-1-64803-770-2

Westwood Books Publishing LLC
11416 SW Aventino Drive
Port Saint Lucie, FL 34987

www.westwoodbookspublishing.com

An Old Texan's Poetry

Poetry in this book covers many aspects of:

1. Texas
2. Qualities of character
3. Life's experiences
4. Human emotions
5. God's directives

Dedication

All poetry found in this book is dedicated to Laura Jo Holley Jackson. And to our children: Roy James, Lisa, Mark, and Luke.

For 53 years, she was with me, a talented, wonderful wife, and my anchor in life.

She taught me so very much about life, living, and loving people.

She shall greet me at the gates of heaven.

The Old Texan
Roy Buford Jackson
Granbury, Texas

Message to the reader

Poetry can be informative.
Poetry can be beautiful.
Poetry can be inspiring.
Poetry can be uplifting.
Poetry can enhance love.
Poetry can enrich life.
Poetry can help uncovering your soul.
Poetry can aid in loss of loved ones.
Poetry can be one of God's greatest gifts to you.

From the Old Texan

Contents

Acknowledgment

As an Old Texan, who composed these poems, acknowledgment is due to my main editor, confident, and friend, Dave Werling (Rte. UASF).

Dave has traveled the world in his military service career, and has been a solid critic of my literary efforts.

His view of me (given in his attempt at poetry) provides a bit of humor, and follows as the end of this acknowledgment.

I also want to thank my only daughter, Laura Elizabeth Jackson, for final cleanup editing efforts and suggestions.

I have not always followed their advice, so any form, format, content, or mistakes of any kind are mine, and mine alone.

I hope that you enjoy in many ways an Old Texan's Poetry.

You are encouraged to send comments to my Internet address, r8jcks@aol.com.

May God Bless you and yours!!

The Old Texan

You may order online either hardcover, paperback cover, or download versions of this book from www.westwoodbookspublishing.com

My friend Roy

What shall we call a "Roy?",
Is it "a king or a boy?".

Google says it's "Irish for Red",
I say it's "someone twas hit on the head".

Others say No!
It a name of renown.

We know it from South. Side Chicago,
In a song called Le Roy Brown.

This poem is for my friend Roy Jackson,
Its long but not up to a chanson.

It isn't an epic, that's not in its nature,
It's writ for a scrivener, a user of paper.

Whole glades are cut down for this man's play,
Tons of ink for his pen, wait on the quay.

Poems are writ for whatever reason,
And I say lay with lot's tease'n.

And there this preamble verse ends,
Now to the rest of the poem to see where it ends.

Roy lives in space, where we haven't been,
A tera formed Mars and worlds without end.

Spirit, then soul and time without end,
Sentience in the womb, fancy beyond ken.

His vision now soars past suns turned to coals,
A Ponce de Leon, seeks the well of souls.

At our table he lays out "the first and the last",
Of all things round which his net he has cast.

Today it's iron heroes on horses posed fine,
(Now ridden by pigeons and squirrels),
Jacked from their pediments by rascally swine,
(Fore whom we cast pearls).

Then Roy pummels the air with invective most dire,
With the 'rasure of history, sees demise of the shire.

Mid meal we'll stall and ponder, pause and sit,
As my friend is large from eating more than a lit.

But he's now on the charge, getting back on his feet,
His spirit is willing, tho flesh is some weak.

See now - he digs deep! You know, he's still a Marine!
He's lost scores of pounds, and startin' to look mean,
(By that I mean, less broad in the beam).

He smiles, says his spirit is kind, most gentle of face,
But Iran's bag of our drone in international space,
Brings strong remonstrance, furled brow, wisdom for 'the chief,
"Give them a lesson! Bombs and hellfire without relief!".

Roy strews counsel without asking for plunder,
Knowledge blown wide with wisdom-like thunder.

But pause now, let's consider the many parts of this sage.

Quantum physics, folk wisdom, statecraft'.

He covers the stage.

But beyond these gifts of superior getting.

He has a gift still more surpassing!
He has, he says, the gift of women magnetizing.

This gift finds him to be to women a magnet,
He says, "ladies find me a real Plantagenet".

He speaks further and now cracks wise,
He says women are the superior sex. certainly not frail,
His grandmother, his mother too, o'er their men prevailed.

As he preaches on women, wind fills his sails,
And his torrent of words makes whales of gales.

But tough women merit his caution and scorn,
As he feels that men to their weakness are born.

Roy says that women, are sneaky with guile,
Says that Man's a sucker for Woman's wile.

He tells a story from women of old.

One was quite nasty the other quite bold.

Jezebel's vineyard cost the life of a man,
Bathsheba found luck in a bathing pan.

But then Jezebel took a step all too high,
For Bathsheba's step up a man had to die.

We look about now and what do
we see?
The Chairman Pelosi and the
Ms. AOC.

As one quite old, AOC shines
bright new.

20 20 shows what they think of
this crew.

Beware Women he says are the
superior sex,
God made men simple but
women complex.

or
On TV we see what's going around,
They say Donald Trump is losing
ground.

Though to his challengers he
gives a smile,
He might lose to a gal by a
country mile.

Proof shows there's more men by the pound,
But fewer last long, they don't hang around.

Roy points to the numbers, in the math he finds truth,
He says "Men die early, women just get long in the tooth".

In contrast to them, men are simple, lumbered by nature,
Women multi task, raise kids, the real movers and shakers.

I believe he blames Eve for leading Adam astray,
By proffering her love apple at the end of the day.

My friend writes poems for with words he's unique,
They flow from his pen - some straight, others oblique.

They walk, wander and tumble but rarely are terse,
He's been touched by the muse of meandering verse.

Roy speaks with authority; he says "it's all fact!",
But I know its a ploy to see how others react.

(Roy responds and talks me down).

"Don't give me no Jack! I got it all writ down!"
That makes it fact! And I ain't no Le Roy Brown!"

"Remember this: I'm magnetic, I ride the red dragon!"
Instead of - "Hey you! - address me as 'le roi' Jackson!"

David Werling
July, 2019

1

Our Beginning and Ending

As I remember meeting you,
For the very first time,
I sensed someone very fine,
Deep feelings clouded my mind.

It was the beginning,
This nearness of you,
It was not quite clear,
As you smiled so dear.

My heart seemed to swell,
With feelings never felt before,
Because I was with you,
My life felt completed now.

After that I could not rest,
Until we were meeting again,
I knew without a doubt,
You were my soul mate to be.

My wife beloved to be,
Never after could I rest,
As I pursued you for marriage,
Until it became true.

I always knew God sent you,
You were meant to be mine,
Sharing life's ups and downs,
With I who needed you so.

You stood by my side,
Through good and bad,
Building a family wanted by us,
Becoming soul mates without a doubt.

My pride in you was always great,
My need for you never lost,
My love for you just grew and grew,
As years together past quickly by.

And when God called you back,
To early my dearest I know,
My heart broke apart with sorrow,
Anguish damaged my soul.

I had not enough time to say goodbye,
Nor provided enough final support I know,
At times my decisions were wrong,
But I always had you in my mind.

So I ask before God and man,
Forgive me for any disappointments,
Forgive me my love, forgive me,
I beg of thee, forgive me.

I still grieve to have you here,
Again near to me dearest one,
But alas that is not to be so,
Until God Himself calls me home.

I pray, hope, plead with you,
That at that time,
We will be allowed by God,
To be together, forever more.

2

Fear No Terror

Life is short,
Hopefully sweet,
Full of love,
Challenge, fulfillment.

Terror is horror,
Destruction,
Desolation,
Death itself.

Fear is fright,
Chaos, reason lost,
Logic destroyed,
Evil in charge.

Freedom is to think,
With clear response,
Proper strength applied,
Which always defeats fear.

Those that produce,
Nothing but fear,
Terror, hatred,
Shall always lose.

As they offer nothing,
Just destructive waste,
And a life filled,
With emptiness of spirit.

Only fleeting feelings,
Based on terror,
With mindless horrors,
Empty of love.

No true path,
To God's eternity,
Nor love, life,
Only terror itself.

So fear not terror,
Those that espouse,
All such false doctrines,
For power.

For they cannot last,
Here on this earth,
Which God made for us,
Including all our freedoms.

He made it for us,
To build upon,
To achieve,
To improve, learn.

To understand,
Ourselves, others,
Our soul's growth,
Our love for all.

As we reach out,
Into His infinity.
Fear no terror,
Never ever.

Nor fear no one,
Spreading such horrors,
As they in time,
Surely have lost all.

Life's wonders of living,
Have been thrown away,
God's blessings included,
His love for all lost, lost, lost.

All rights, privileges,
Even love, life, itself,
Creating mindless horrors,
Cruelties, stupidities, beyond measure.

Our human spirit needs,
Indeed demands,
Thrives upon,
A love of God and each other.

Our human values,
Requires common sense,
Applied equality a must,
With others always in mind.

Our humanity needs,
Peaceful growth,
Tolerances,
Freedoms for all.

Understanding that our souls,
Must have God's blessings,
Which excludes,
Fearing any terror, evermore.

3

The Texas Roadrunner

O' Roadrunner, Roadrunner,
Why not fly into the sky,
Instead you run, turn,
Quicker than the eye.

O' Roadrunner, Roadrunner,
You have wings as other birds,
Should you not soar,
Into the sky same as they?

O' Roadrunner, Roadrunner,
You just run, run, run,
Almost faster than a gun shot,
Under the Texas hot sun.

O' Roadrunner, Roadrunner,
In Texas scorched country side,
Drab colors your feathers are,
Well matched to help you hide.

O' Roadrunner, Roadrunner,
Instead of the Mockingbird,
Its beautiful songs one hears,
Just what use are you?

O' Roadrunner, Roadrunner,
You cannot sing,
Have not beauty,
Nor even fly.

You just hide,
Blending into Texas country side,
Running, running, running,
Or just glide, glide, gliding bye.

4

Golden Days

Life has, at random times,
Days that become golden memories,
Never forgotten,
Remembered, a perfect picture.

Such days are golden,
Full of flavor,
To be tasted again,
Over the passing years.

Accomplishments reached,
Successes achieved,
Difficult odds overcome,
Savored once again.

Loved ones, friends,
Circumstances, come to mind,
Trials, troubles,
And travails encountered.

All remembered, never forgotten,
Flavoring life's' experiences,
Memories never forgotten,
Becoming golden memories recalled.

Failures can be treasured memories,
Recalled when needed,
The meaning of living,
Hard lessons remembered.

Each meant to instruct,
Learned from, valued later,
A reference, a guide,
On the time line each of us walk.

Such memories saved,
Good, bad, with recall,
Can be become useful,
Indeed, valuable for you.

Feeling life again,
Instructive growth,
Maturing one's soul,
Needed by all.

Once again recalled,
To be savored,
Tasted, felt, used again,
Not to be forgotten, indeed Golden Days!

5

My Eternal Shepherd

You are my eternal shepherd,
My Lord God,
Watching over my life,
Always close by.

As my allotted sands of time,
Nears completion of its run,
You will welcome me at the gates,
Into Your timeless eternal grace.

At that moment,
I shall be met by your angels,
To escort my eternal soul,
Through the gates into Your heaven.

My book of life,
Lived on earth,
Shall be read,
Accepted and finally filed.

My passed loved ones,
Shall greet me once more,
Taking my soul,
Into their eternal embrace.

I shall have finished my swim,
Through the waters of life,
Given to me by You O God,
And begin my eternal bliss.

Surrounded by unbounded love,
As heaven unfolds unending wonders,
Eternity with my loved ones,
And with You, my Eternal Shepherd.

6

Life's Tides

As each life is being lived,
And allotted years are used,
One by one they pass,
A realization may occur.

Not to all,
Only to a perceptive few,
That each life has "tides",
Just as the oceans have.

High "tides",
Low "tides",
Created by "gravity of life ",
Each "tide" expected or unexpected.

To keep "afloat",
One should be prepared,
To keep their "ship of life",
On an even "keel".

Some are called "challenge of living",
Others "the way things are",
Or just "plain luck",
Most say "that's life".

A few will reason,
Analyze,
Judge,
Acting to keep even their life's "keel".

One must be carefully aware,
Doing what is needed,
To keep in control,
As "life's tides" ebb and flow.

In each life,
Such "tides" will occur,
With high or low waves to endure,
They always shall pass.

Smooth "tides" come again,
Life perfect once more,
Gentle waves so loved,
With sunshine from above.

So life is challenging,
From its start to finish,
Its "tides" a loving gift,
From God to you.

Why Give Thanks

One must remember,
Give thanks for your life,
God has provided for you,
On every day of each year.

Not just on Thanksgiving,
A special day set aside,
For such all know,
But every day given to you.

For all days of life lived,
On your allotted time line,
Give thanks joyfully,
Confidently, gratefully.

For the loves of your life,
For one's spouse, one's children,
For one's family, one's friends,
All those so near and so dear.

For friends long lost,
Friends new,
Friends past
Friends present.

For neighbors,
Fellow workers,
Those liked or disliked,
Those loved or not.

Indeed, all are provided,
Or not provided,
In your life,
By God for a purpose.

God Himself knows,
By immeasurable arrangements,
He makes just for you,
So thank Him.

Because He is challenging you,
Your growth,
Readying you,
For your eternal life to come.

Measuring you,
For your crown of stars,
Made by the Good Shepard,
Just for you.

All that really matters,
Is how your allotted time,
Was used by you,
Following His commands.

Your challenges handled,
Your crises met,
Your considerations made,
Your help provided to others.

Were lives enhanced,
Was society bettered,
Was mankind advanced,
Was love given to all?

Nothing else matters,
But love and help you gave,
Your thanks given,
And your growth achieved.

All "stuff" stays,
Your body, your money,
All properties, everything,
As all just on "loan" by God.

Nothing taken to heaven,
Just your love,
Your memories,
And your eternal soul.

So take care,
While living your life,
Your allotted time here,
Be thankful, as God provides.

Our Cup

Our days of Spring,
So long ago,
Were so very bold,
Now grown old.

We were filled with youth,
Vigor, boundless health,
Energy, looking forward,
To a lasting love together.

Life had no end,
All was goodness,
You were my cup of love,
I yours.

Then our days of Summer came,
Days magnified many times,
Our cup of happiness complete,
Over flowing with love.

Life became full,
Mine full of you,
I was blessed,
With your love for me.

Again the seasons changed,
Our Fall days made entry,
With love, children,
Our family accomplished.

Life had been fulfilled,
For me overflowing,
You were the one,
Filling our cup.

Winter's Golden days now are here,
With a luster of our life well lived,
Full is our cup of love,
With memories of each bygone year.

All held close, so dear, by me,
Remembered lovingly, our filled cup,
Which you filled for me,
Knowing you are safe, in God's eternal car

9

The Red Rose

Perhaps the most beautiful flower,
Is the perfect red rose,
As it conveys our love an so much more,
Of all that life means.

To our spouse,
Our soul mate,
God's greatest gift,
Of all that life means.

To our children,
Caring hopes and dreams,
Into their life yet unknown,
Of all that life means.

As each petal of it unfolds,
Its pure perfume of life,
No other flower can match,
Of all that life means.

Its overwhelming scent,
Bringing bursts of emotions,
Sensed so rarely otherwise,
Of all that life means

Filling the air with overwhelming scent,
Bringing bursts of emotions,
Sensed so rarely otherwise,
Of all that life means.

Forgotten pleasures,
Memories long lost in our past,
So wonderfully present again,
Of all that life means.

Its unfolding petals,
Breathtaking taking in beauty,
A message seen completely,
Of all that life means.

Conveying the best life offers,
Being loved,
Being fulfilled,
Of all that life means.

Only such beauty of one's love to another.
Shown by the perfect red rose,
From giver to receiver,
Shows all that life means.

10

Found Again

As years pass,
Old friends,
Acquaintances,
Family members gone.

Buried,
Vanished,
Forgotten,
In faded time,

Yet, they were loved,
Needed,
Required,
For living life.

Years become decades,
Times passes,
Changes occur,
Memories are stored.

Not lost forever,
Hopefully,
Good remembered,
Bad forgotten.

Time can heal,
Faults, mistakes,
Disagreements,
Conflicts.

When recalled,
All had become shadows,
Lost in time,
Now found once more.

All remembered,
As perhaps they were,
Never to be relived,
When found again.

But loving such memories,
Remembering,
Remembering,
Loved ones, never ever lost at all.

11

Always Hope

As years pass,
Former friends,
Acquaintances,
Family members lost,
Hope remains.

Memories vanish,
Even forgotten,
Memories dim,
Within shadows of time,
Hope endures.

Memories are loved,
Needed,
Treasured,
Required for life fully lived,
Hope recalls.

As time passes,
Life's changes require,
Such memories,
Be stored away,
Hope stays.

Not lost forever,
Recalled,
Good remembered,
Bad forgotten,
Hope remembers.

Time heals,
Faults,
Disagreements,
Perhaps conflicts,
Hope heals.

Good should be recalled,
Forgiveness given,
Differences erased,
In thoughts of times passed,
Hope repairs.

Hope never lost,
Found in hugs,
Embraces courage,
Leads to better times,
Hope enhances.

So always hope,
Remember the good,
As life moves forward,
So remember,
Always hope.

Your Birthday

May this day of days,
Always bring back,
Your life's best,
Its sweetest memories,
On your day of days.

May it always shine,
With bright happiness,
Upon your life,
With blessings upon your soul,
On your day of days.

May you savor the good,
Tasting once more again,
Of your life well lived,
The best of your years,
On your day of days.

And may you always,
Have joy again and again,
Year after blessed year,
As your life unfolds,
On your day of days.

Happy Birthday!!

13

God's Poetry

Every time you look,
Into the dark night sky,
His celestial rhymes,
Of galaxies shine,
Look, behold, I say.

So unbelievable close,
The beautiful star filled sky,
Yet so very far, far, far.
Far away. are they,
Wonder, behold, I say.

Just reach out,
Just touch same,
But alas they are,
Light years away,
Understand, behold, I say.

Vast, beautiful beyond measure,
Inspiring in its celestial glory,
Beyond belief,
God's own poetry certainly is,
Remember, behold, I say.

Our Milky Way,
Just a small part of same,
Crossing the night sky,
Inspiring in it's beauty,
Enjoy, behold, I say.

Reaching horizon to horizon,
Lighting up the night sky,
Its brilliant stars,
All beyond counting,
Think, behold, I say.

Showing His glorious creation,
His infinite universe unbounded,
His poetry in motion,
Awe inspiring,
Accept, behold, I say.

Filling your soul,
Life giving,
Beyond belief,
God's very own poetry,
Beautiful, behold, I say.

His poetry extends,
Throughout our known universe,
Now expanding,
Still being created,
Infinity, behold, I say.

Each one of billions of galaxies,
Contains many black holes,
Millions of stars, planets,
With asteroids uncounted,
Unnumbered, behold I say.

Even comets show us,
Their brilliant fiery tails,
As they cross our night sky,
Stunning all that see,
Searching, behold, I say.

All sorts of celestial bodies,
In gravity's eternal sway,
Unfolding eternity to us all,
God's own poetry,
Behold, behold, again, and again, I say.

Your Awakenings

Before birth awareness starts,
Another new beginning,
A separate human being,
A new life to be lived.

Life comprises four awakenings,
Each disturbing,
Surprising,
Each at different times.

Your four awakenings,
Physical, mental,
Emotional,
Spiritual.

Each awareness of same,
Occurs at appointed times,
As life progresses,
Four separate awakenings.

Each life separate,
Distinct,
Unique,
Different.

But each life,
In every aspect,
Similar to all,
Who experience this existence.

Physical awareness,
Begins when the womb is left,
Body sensations felt,
A separate life begun.

Mental awareness is next,
Hunger experienced,
Warmth required,
Sleep necessary.

Growth begins,
Memory has begun,
The brain functions,
Learning processes starts.

Then emotions emerge,
Personal awareness,
Frustrations,
Human feelings shown.

Such feelings,
Love first,
Hate last,
Others, as life moves forward.

Spiritual awareness is last,
Of ones' own soul,
Placed by God,
Your eternal part of life.

Such has been seen,
By mankind's great philosophers,
As God's total summation of your life,
Your soul, your eternal part, your forever awaking.

15

Life's Flavors

Life consists of "flavors",
Which may be tasted,
Some are tangible,
Others just sensed.

Some flavors you know,
Some unknown,
Successes encountered,
Failures that happen.

Some flavors bring happiness,
Some sadness,
Some expected,
Many just surprise.

Life's flavors constantly change,
From beginning to end,
Each flavor adding,
To experiences remembered.

Perhaps a sweet tasting flavor,
Delightful,
Inspiring,
Enjoyable beyond measure.

Or a bitter tasting flavor,
With dire costs,
Requiring actions,
Corrections needed.

Sometimes flavors mix,
A warning of sorts,
Making a hard decision,
Causing change in life.

A flavor for better, one hopes,
Done in time,
Damage avoided,
Joy restored.

Life's flavors flux,
As one's time flows on,
With new challenges,
Always occurring.

Perhaps life is about such flavoring,
Reacting to circumstances,
From moment to moment,
God Himself flavoring your eternal soul.

Reflections

Time for reflections,
Remembered occurrences,
Carefully savored,
Tasting your past once more.

Such reflections,
Remembered again,
Seen with truth, clearness, honestly,
Are shown in your life's mirror.

Past times cannot be changed,
Past mistakes corrected,
Past hurts removed,
Past injuries erased.

Reflections clearly seen,
Of what was done is done,
Reflections cannot be changed,
In your life's mirror.

However, reflections remembered,
Thankfully, hopefully, most,
Filled with sweetness and joy,
Can be savored once more.

Loves remembered,
Family and friends,
Achievements made,
Life's victories recalled.

God's blessing received,
Remembered moments,
Mistakes corrected,
Opportunities sized.

Love given to you,
Or love given by you,
Remembering the good, not the bad,
Reflections all, just reflections, reflections I say.

No Next Time

O My soul,
My eternal self,
Placed in my body,
While in the womb.

Made by God Himself.
Taken from His Well of Souls,
Just for me,
For all eternity.

My time on this earth,
Must be well lived I know,
As I learn life's lessons,
Performing His assigned tasks.

Upon completing same,
While on His earth.
My soul should have grown,
As God surely intends it to be.

As our Savior told us,
There is no next time,
His lessons were clear,
His teachings understood.

There is no excuse,
Not to know,
Each here has one time only,
For their soul to grow.

I have tried,
I have made mistakes,
I have faults, I know,
Forgiveness, I humbly ask, from Thee.

So I pray, as my ending years are here,
That when my "Book of Life",
When read at heaven's gate,
Will close with a earned, "Well done, My child".

So Silently, Time Flows By

An angel's wings have no sound,
We hear not a slightest flutter,
God's attendants performing tasks,
As time flows silently by.

Done to perfection,
Invisible to our senses,
Each completed with care,
As time flows silently by.

Love also flows,
Good done,
Harm repaired,
As time flows silently by.

God's plans can change,
Souls shaken.
Destinies designated,
As time flows silently by.

Time for us flows,
Much like water,
Sometimes fast, sometimes slow,
As time flows silently by.

Only flowing forward,
Never flowing backward,
What's done is done,
As time flows silently by.

Never to be undone,
Never to be changed,
All done and accountable to God,
As time flows silently by.

Only God Himself,
His angels in attendance,
May travel time's infinite length,
As time flows silently by.

God can stop time,
Start time,
Change time,
As time flows silently by.

We can never change,
The silent flow of time,
Only to travel forward,
As time flows silently by.

When Your Day is Done

When your day is done,
Rest will surely come,
When your day is done,
All struggles shall cease.

When your day is done,
Concerns are put aside,
When your day is done,
Night falls once again.

When your day is done,
Your mind goes silent,
When your day is done,
Your body craves rest.

When your day is done,
Dreams can come,
When your day is done,
Night falls once again.

When your day is done,
Reminiscences may return,
When your day is done,
Past occurrences become dear.

When your day is done,
Love of all remembered,
When your day is done,
Night falls once again.

When your day is done,
Time shall cease,
When your day is done,
New existence imagined.

When your day is done,
One nearer eternity,
When your day is done,
Night falls once again.

When your day is done,
Strange sensations felt,
When your day is done,
Angels may be heard.

When your day is done,
God Himself says, "Well Done",
When your final day is done,
Eternal night falls for evermore.

Some of Life's Wonders

All who have ever lived,
Those living now,
Those yet to come,
Will have experienced wonders.

Many may not realize,
But with a bit of wisdom,
They shall remember,
When each occurred.

Among life's many wonders,
The immense power of love,
Love for others,
For family, friends, country.

Love cannot be explained,
It's a driving power,
Felt so deeply,
In one's soul.

The drive to live,
Not to leave this life,
To live another day,
Feeling the flow of life itself.

Experiencing the senses,
Touch, smell, taste, hearing, sight,
All makes living,
A completed day.

Even speaking, sharing moments,
Conveying thoughts, emotions,
Transferring ideas, good or bad,
Makes living wonderful.

To wonder on a clear night's sky,
Looking up at uncountable stars,
Clearly seen, yet so far far away.
Stirs life's wonders to its depths.

Perhaps seen alone,
Or clustered in galaxies,
Beautiful beyond measure,
All following gravity's laws.

Beautiful is a child's smile,
Enjoyment of life itself,
Whether at play, school, church, or home,
Radiates wonders of living love.

Such a smile,
Coupled with laughter,
Reminds one once again,
Life's wonders shall continue.

The final wonder of life,
Is our eternal soul,
Given by God to each,
Because He loves us so

21

To Return Home Again

Returning home again,
Is a dream, a wish,
Many have some time,
Home will not be the same.

Never to be done,
Time marches on,
Never into the past,
Home will not be the same.

Time does not pass "home" by,
Change is always occurring,
Sometimes fast, sometimes slow,
Home will not be the same.

Change does vary,
As time marches forward,
But always forward,
Home will not be the same.

Returning home is but a dream,
Perhaps to right past wrongs,
To modify, to correct,
Home will not be the same.

You and others have changed,
Life itself has moved,
The clock of life keeps ticking,
Home will not be the same.

God's Joys Once More

Life has many joys,
Which God provides,
Remembering a face gone,
Part of God's given joys.

Recalling a beautiful sky,
Or child born,
Hugs of love,
Part of God's given joys.

Hearing music,
Stiring emotions,
Feeling the eternal soul,
Part of God's given joys.

Love of remembrances,
Of events long past,
Hearing a voice long stilled,
Part of God's given joys.

Touch of a loved one,
Stored in life's files,
Perhaps a gentle caress,
Part of God's given joys.

Thoughts lost in time,
Recalled once more,
Not forgotten,
Part of God's given joys.

Treasured moments,
Wonderful recalled memories,
Never lost, just misplaced,
Part of God's given joys.

Dimmed by time,
But remembered now,
To be savored again,
Part of God's given joys.

Such reminiscences stored away,
Just part of one's life,
Brought back again,
Just part of God's given joys.

23-1

My Plea for Him, O God Above

O God above us all,
Hear my plea I beg of Thee,
Just listen to me,
Let him stay I ask of Thee.

O God above us all,
We need him here,
So heal him, I pray,
Help him now for all to see.

O God above us all,
Again I plead for him,
Make him well again,
For we need him so.

O God above us all,
I ask of Thee, on bended knee,
He is so young to go,
And we love him so.

O God above us all,
If he is to leave,
Please treat him gently,
As I bid him a final goodbye.

O God above us all,
Welcome him into your eternal home,
And keep him eternally safe,
I humbly ask of Thee.

My Plea for Her, O God Above

O God above us all,
Hear my plea, I beg of Thee,
Just listen to me,
Let her stay, I ask of Thee.

O God above us all,
We need her here,
So heal her for me,
Help her now, for all to see.

O God above us all,
Again I plead for her,
Make her well for us again,
For we need her so.

O God above us all,
I beg of Thee, on bended knee,
She is wanted, so needed here,
And we love her so.

O God above us all,
If she is to leave us now,
Please treat her gently,
As I bid her a final goodbye.

O God above us all,
Welcome her into your eternal home,
And keep her eternally safe,
I humbly ask of Thee.

The Texas Armadillo

A strange creature,
Found in Texas,
Out of place,
Time has forgotten,
Did time forget you?

A living critter or a beast,
From eons past,
A miniature copy,
Of what it once was,
Fearsome so long ago?

This strange creature,
The Texas Armadillo,
Small in size,
Long in snout,
Why such a hose for a nose?

It has large ears,
Over lapping body armor,
Like a tiny tank,
Big as a large cat,
But where is your fur?

Sporting digging claws.
On each foot it has,
To dig grubs, worms,
Or even small insects, roots,
Why such stuff you eat?

Digging into the earth,
At such frighting speed,
Leaving large holes,
Causing great damage.
Do you care at all?

Each hole can be danger,
To cattle, horses, and such,
Your previous hiding places,
Which must be filled,
Why such a pest you be?

One established fact,
Adds to its reputation,
Besides us humans,
It can carry leprosy,
From biblical days perhaps?

Another, the female version,
Always has four offspring,
All at the same time,
All of the same sex,
Creating mystery to solve?

Male or female,
Never mixed,
No one knows why,
So strange a fact,
A puzzle for us?

Questions arise,
How she knows,
Just which is needed,
Male, or female,
Tell us, if you can?

Why always four,
Of the same sex,
Plus, its a nocturnal animal,
Usually seen at night,
Why hiding all day long?

Shy it is,
Always afraid,
A ancient survivalist,
Still with us,
Our Texas Armadillo.

A creature gentle in nature,
Found in groups,
Harmless, nonaggression,
Small, fast, a digger of earths,
Digging, digging, always digging.

It has found a place,
In great Texas lore,
Always know for sure,
Strange as it all seems,
The Texas Armadillo.

The Texas Diamond Back

A dangerous snake,
In all of Texas,
Emits a loud rattling sound,
When angered,
Its strike most deadly bound.

Coiled, ready, mad,
In powerful striking position,
Feared rightly so,
The Texas Diamond Back,
A sourage to any and all.

Its viper head,
Two long fangs exposed,
Reared back,
To deliver death with speed,
Faster than can be seen.

Unleashing poisoned venom,
Into any in reach,
Uncoiling to full length,
Striking, killing if it can,
Death dealing bound.

Best be aware,
Hear its warning rattle,
Step quickly out of range,
Then go on your way,
As quickly as one can.

However it has use,
As it eats field mice, rats,
Even lizards, and other pests,
Cleaning Texas of same,
Nature at its best and worst.

Naturalists beg all,
Not to abuse, kill,
Texas needs such a snake
For natures balance,
They tell all.

However, its a hidden danger.
Anywhere encountered,
Give it wide berth,
Keep from its striking range,
Your girth for sure.

Death carried in its venom,
Delivered by fangs,
Always avoid for sure,
Murderous death, pain, hurt,
The great Texas Diamond Back.

26

The Texas Horned Toad

A small horned,
Dry land reptile,
Totally harmless "toad",
Is the Texas Horned Toad.

Now vanishing across Texas,
At unbelievable rapid rates.
Due to fire ants, pesticides,
Human encroachment as well.

Disappearing from Texas,
Placed on endangered lists,
Needing to be saved.
Is our Texas Horned Toad.

Older Texans remember,
Having such a cute pet,
Small horns on each side of its head.
Gentle, harmless, Texas' tame reptile.

Fast in movement,
Shy, held in your hand.
Insects their food,
Usually ants, or other insects.

Though not "fire ants",
Destructive, deadly,
Originally from Brazil,
Now killing our Texas Horned Toad.

Pesticides like DDT,
Have taken its toll,
Our growing Texas cities,
Also have done so too.

Time now running out,
For saving our gentle horned toad,
Friend to Texas for uncountable years,
Perhaps soon, just leaving Texans in tears.

27

The Texas Longhorn

A great magnificent beast,
The Texas Longhorn cow,
Growing extreme long horns,
Many feet wide tip to tip,
The famed Texas Longhorn.

Meat of the Texas Longhorn,
Very tough to eat,
Today's breeds, Herefords, Angus,
Now replace past great herds,
Of the famed Texas Longhorns.

Mean tempered, unpredictable,
With size matching any cattle seen,
Be careful approaching same,
Danger lurks in such as they,
The famed Texas Longhorn.

Its temper without cause,
Very quickly aroused,
Immense size, speed, strength,
Armed with such wicked horns,
The famed Texas Longhorn.

Causes damage beyond belief,
It stomps, crushes, or can spear,
With sharp tipped long horns,
Reaching out to impale all,
The famed Texas Longhorn.

Indeed, other animals give way,
To live another day,
Running every such way,
Avoiding such hoofed fury,
From the famed Texas Longhorn.

Give this huge bovine,
A long horned monster,
Venting his temper,
Plenty of empty space,
The famed Texas Longhorn.

Only a trained Texas cowboy,
With nerves of steel,
On horseback of course,
Can somewhat control it,
The famed Texas Longhorn.

The Texas Copperhead

Among Texas's deadly snakes,
Is the copperhead,
Small, quick, venomous,
Is this potential killer,
The Texas Copperhead.

Smelling like copper metal,
Carrying hard fangs to match,
Hiding about, no warning ever,
Waiting to strike any and all,
The Texas Copperhead.

Just potential death waiting,
Lurking about, small,
Deadly, and quick,
No rattles, no coiling required,
The Texas Copperhead.

Hidden under or behind anything,
Very poisonous, rarely seen,
Usually smelled first, but being close,
Able to deliver death's pick,
The Texas Copperhead.

The copperhead thankfully,
Not widespread as rattlesnakes,
Nor as aggressive,
Unless uncovered from hiding,
The Texas Copperhead.

Remember copperheads smell,
Giving intended victims,
Chance to avoid it,
And its venomous strike,
The Texas Copperhead.

Is very wise to give,
Any copperhead wide berth,
Unless a long handled hoe,
Or other garden tool available,
To kill the Texas Copperhead.

Quickly chop it to pieces,
Avoiding his poisons delivery,
Such actions result in its death,
Not yours, when in its territory,
The Texas Copperhead.

The Texas Coral Snake

Texas's most deadly snake,
Just beautiful to behold,
Carrying very bold colors,
Alternating red and yellow bands,
The Texas Coral Snake.

Very small, looking harmless,
Not quick in movement,
Unable to strike, just chew,
Less known as Texas rattlers,
The Texas Coral Snake.

Member of the cobra family,
Deadly they are,
Delivering end to life,
So look about if seen,
The Texas Coral Snake.

Exquisite in coloring,
Small in length,
Danger in extreme,
Can kill any in its way,
The Texas Coral Snake.

Mimicked by a harmless,
But again beautiful one,
The Texas king snake,
Displaying red and black,
In alternating bands.

A trick of nature,
Self protection, by the king,
Masquerading as a coral,
So all may believe it to be,
The Texas Coral Snake,

Just remember a rime,
Developed by Texans back in time,
"Red and Yellow, kill a fellow",
"Red and Black, friend of Jack",
To know the Texas Coral Snake.

Such a rhyme known by you,
Keeps one aware,
Of the coral snake,
And not get in a life ending bind,
Due to The Texas Coral Snake.

30

The Texas Red Ants

In all parts of Texas,
Many ants are known,
Whenever such appears,
Beware such crawlers.
They may be Texas' Red Ants.

If large, colored red, aggressive,
Quickly back away,
Avoiding painful stings,
Felt to your very bones,
By Texas' Red Ants.

Such ants well known,
Found in great mounds,
Around the entire state,
Dangers to all life,
These Texas' Red Ants.

Ruining farm land, cattle land,
Hurting all with their swarms,
Killing insects, horned toads,
Small things, even people,
Beware of Texas' Red Ants.

A small child, innocent as can be,
Walking upon its mound,
Instantly swarmed, stung repeatedly,
helpless, unable to move.
By Texas' Red Ants.

Encountering such danger,
Its hard to think,
In a fiery agony,
Help needed now,
Because of Texas' Red Ants.

Found in city, farms, ranches,
Forest, or any unexpected places,
Building their mounds,
Always swarming about,
Are Texas Red Ants.

Always active,
Hurtful to all,
Delivering a unexpected danger,
Even death, if they can,
Beware, avoid Texas Red Ants.

Texas Turkey Buzzard

Why do you fly so high,
Just floating by,
So lazy high in the sky,
Looking down, looking down,
Why?

Always seen by all,
But never noise made,
Silently carried by the winds,
Always looking down,
Why?

In flocks circling high above,
Ever expanding numbers occur,
Coming lower an hovering about,
Looking down, tell us,
Why?

The answer must be hunger,
Driven by a super sense of smell,
Nature needs such a cleaner,
Always looking down,
That's why.

With a black, repulsive,
Death like appearance,
When seen on the ground,
Eating all dead things found,
All decaying, just laying about.

The stomach you must have,
With an appetite to match,
Eating any thing dead,
Or perhaps just about,
Yet a Texas bird you are.

Serving all below,
By floating so high above,
Just filling natures needs,
Waiting to feed,
Thank you, Turkey Buzzard, for keeping Texas clean.

The Texas Hound Dog

Always a hound dog needed,
Indispensable when hunting,
Even before the Texas Republic began,
A four footed trusted friend,
The Texas Hound Dog.

His nose, hunting instincts,
Friendship,
Always on the watch,
Defines him a guardian,
The Texas Hound Dog.

On the hunt his instincts,
Beyond fault,
Ever watchful,
Always ahead of all,
The Texas Hound Dog.

All senses alert,
Conveying ahead,
Howling, growling, leading,
Baying for all to hear,
The Texas Hound Dog.

Trained to trail.
Smelling scents of game,
He ranges about,
Taking all things in,
The Texas Hound Dog.

So trusted can he be,
A hunter assured to win,
Whatever the game,
It will be found,
By the Texas Hound Dog.

At the end of the day,
As all are gathered about,
The family knows no doubt,
His place in our lore,
The Texas Hound Dog.

Such a great companion,
Devoted friend, protector,
Reliable beyond measure,
Even to his death,
The Texas Hound Dog.

Watching all with care,
In his "pack" we know,
More than a valued animal,
Faithful beyond measure,
The Texas Hound Dog.

Known as a trusted friend,
Watchful, helpful,
Dependable,
A true family member,
Our Texas Hound Dog.

33

The Texas Mesquite Tree

Found all over in Texas,
A strange almost useless thing,
A tree covering parts of our state,
Called the Texas curse,
Texas' Mesquite Tree.

A tree of little value,
With even less use,
A scrub tree,
A land ruining scourge,
Texas' Mesquite Tree.

Such a tree ruins Texas land,
For ranching, farming,
Taking scarce water resources,
Hard to clear, even burn,
Texas' Mesquite Tree.

Sprouting long hard thorns,
Growing seed pods by dozens,
Spreading root runners,
Dense in numbers,
Texas' Mesquite Tree.

Its thorns penetrate anything,
Hurting horses, cattle,
Trying to eat its pods,
Desperate with hunger,
Texas' Mesquite Tree.

In case of range fire,
Texas Mesquite Tree survives,
It burns, soon recovers,
Even with little water,
Texas' Mesquite Tree.

In case of drought,
It will survive,
Outlasting cactus plants,
Other trees perish,
But not Texas' Mesquite Tree.

To kill it finally,
Texas' Mesquite Tree requires,
Complete digging up,
Including roots, root runners,
Burning all, even its pods.

So clearing is expensive,
Time consuming,
Hard to do,
Apparently, God believed,
Texas required the Texas Mesquite Tree

The Texas Cedar Tree

It is not majestic,
Like mighty redwoods,
Or forests of spruce,
The Texas Cedar Tree.

Nor is it beautiful,
As live oaks,
With hanging moss,
The Texas Cedar Tree.

Neither does it have edible nuts,
As pecan trees,
Or walnut and almond trees,
The Texas Cedar Tree.

It offers very little,
No fruits, or nuts,
Nor a lumber source.
The Texas Cedar Tree.

Nothing can grow,
Under its dense bush like limbs,
Only small animals seek its shade,
Under the Texas Cedar Tree.

It sucks nutrients from the ground,
Drawing moisture from the soil,
Ruins land for farming or ranching,
Does the Texas Cedar Tree.

Birds, deer, other wild things,
May choose to hide within it,
Penetrating dense foliage of needle like leaves,
Surrounding the Texas Cedar Tree.

It pollinates almost all year long,
Growing purple pods,
Exploding its seeds into the air.
Caused by the Texas Cedar Tree.

Any human being,
Can suffer from same,
With allergy's beyond description,
The Texas Cedar Tree.

Suffering with ever breath taken,
Itching, breathing, sinuses, under attack,
Immune systems fighting back,
The Texas Cedar Tree.

The only use for such a tree,
Is fence posts from its larger limbs,
Or barbecue briquettes, flavoring Texas prime beef,
By the Texas Cedar Tree.

Other than that,
It ruins all land overtaken,
Causing a Texas size problem,
The Texas Cedar Tree.

35

The Texas Tornadoes

Tornadoes occur in Texas,
More than any other state,
Perhaps, four thousand a year,
An average from long records.

In angry, dark cloudy, spinning skies,
A long funnel suddenly drops down,
Randomly descending,
Great in force, in destruction.

A vortex spinning about,
Jumping hither and yonder,
Perhaps above you,
Finally on the ground.

Rips, uproots, tears, renders, breaks,
Shreds, mangles, any thing, even kills,
Reminding Texans nature itself,
Is always in charge.

No matter time of year,
Seasons and reason not count,
A Texas tornado can occur,
Anytime, place, hour of day.

In weather that changes,
On the "drop of a hat",
It can form, drop down,
Or blow by, an go on its way.

But in any case,
If a storm cellar nearby,
Go to same in a flash,
As "quickly as pie"

But seek safety,
Get out of its path,
If you can,
To live for another day.

36

The Texas Thunder Storm

Whenever thick dark clouds are seen,
Rolling in dark anger in the Texas sky,
Obscuring either sun, or a starlit night,
Fair warning nature is providing.
Of a Texas thunder storm being near.

Nature's show begins in brief minutes,
Deadly lightning strikes may soon occur,
Thunderous sounds shakes ones nerves,
Driving icy rain, howling winds, baseball sized hail,
All can be in a Texas thunder storm.

Quickly take cover. if one can,
Be it in farm house, ranch house,
A barn, hopefully well equipped,
On its roof, with a metal rod,
To lesson damage of a Texas thunder storm.

Placed on a structures roof,
Attached to a metal cable,
With the cables other end,
Buried underground, guiding lightning strikes,
To earth, during a Texas thunder storm.

Else life can be lost.
Lighting strikes split trees,
Start range fires, kill cattle,
All life is in its high voltage path,
Produced by a Texas thunder storm.

Homes can be burned to the ground,
Barns, other structures, as well,
Destruction, death, such loss does occur,
Every year, every year, in our great Texas,
Caused by our Texas thunder storms.

Natures thunder storms, especially in Texas,
May contain power to delight,
But death, destruction, costs, do not,
Which Texans know very well,
Having to deal with Texas thunder storms.

Even Texans can be made powerless,
By one of natures common occurrences,
Making our state extremely aware,
Of death, destruction, loss, created by,
The terrible Texas thunder storm.

The Texas People

Texas people,
Either native, or living here,
Have Texas in their blood,
All are wonderful folks.

Texas people are,
Without any doubt,
Some of the finest people,
God ever made.

Placed in Texas,
By God, or choice,
They get things done,
In a common sense way.

Texas people,
Work hard, play hard, live hard,
Endure whatever necessary,
Thanking God, for Texas.

Some say God put His best,
Here in this great state,
Most Texans believe that,
Since extra grit is needed to be a Texan.

Including other traits,
Like determination, foresight,
Willpower, character, energy,
A fighting spirit.

Building Texas character always,
Winning thru to victory,
Facing unbelievable problems.
But never wavering, never, never.

People such as Sam Houston,
Davy Crockett, William Travis,
Juan Seguin, "Deaf" Smith,
Texas heroes, well known.

From fighting the war of Texas Independence,
Against Mexico's Santa Anna,
Despised dictator, tyrant, despot,
Self proclaimed "Napoleon of the West".

Remember the Alamo",
Remember Goliad",
Remember San Jacinto",
All will never be forgotten.

Texas became an independent nation,
A separate country, standing by itself,
Among the world's family of nations,
Known as "The Republic of Texas".

New Mexico, Arizona, Oklahoma,
Plus large parts of Colorado, and Kansas,
Were given up by Texas,
To join the United States of America.

Texas illustrious history,
Illustrates the soul of freedom.
Recalled by those seeking independence,
Against oppression, tyrants, dictators.

Our history also honors our Texas Rangers,
Superb shots, riders, protectors, brave warriors,
Who fought Comanche, Apache, bandits,
Making Texas safe, for settlers, our vast lands.

Today Texas is populated by people,
Representing all races, colors, religions, backgrounds,
Different in heritages, all proud, resilient, with abundant grit,
Our founders would be pleased, as Texans stand tall, always.

The Texas Night Skies

On any clear dark evening,
As one looks up,
At a Texas night sky,
A breath taking sight is seen.

Stars shining so brightly,
From horizon to horizon,
Countless beyond number,
Going into eternity forever.

One may just reach out,
To touch a star,
They seem close,
Yet they are very, very, far away.

Much light in a Texas night sky,
Stars, galaxies, just uncountable,
The Milky Way seen clearly,
Beautiful, inspiring, to all.

However, a full moon,
In a Texas sky, is different,
One sees night another way,
It turns night into day.

Indeed, as each season comes,
And then goes, be alert,
Texas skies can change,
From hour to hour.

From sky blue beautiful,
To dust storms,
To dark tornadoes,
To torrential hail.

So each Texan,
Learns early on,
Watching the Texas sky very carefully,
Its changes so rapidly, whats next to see?

39

The Texas Water Problem

Water means life,
To all in Texas,
Oil, natural gas, cattle, crops,
Only a wealth source,
Texas needs more water.

Texas has abundant land,
But not enough water,
So very much needed,
A wondrous gift, abundant water,
Texas always lacks water.

Water in abundance,
Means livestock lives,
Wildlife flourishes,
All over the state,
Texans have fought over water.

Crops in the fields,
Grown full to harvest,
Life can go on,
For another full year,
Texas needs more water.

Water means people,
Can move forward,
Live without fear,
Of dreaded Texas drought,
Texas must have more water.

Citrus groves will flourish,
In the Rio Grand valley,
Fruitful again another year,
A Texas Harvest in bounty,
If, only if, the Rio Grand river fully flows.

Water means all Texas crops,
Flourishing once again,
Cotton fields full of fluffy bolls,
Corn stalks with full ears for harvest,
Texans knows what abundant water brings.

Water means no dust storms,
Blotting out the beautiful Texas sky.
Choking people with horrid dust,
Every breath hurting one's lungs,
Texans known water means survival.

Water means no dying livestock,
All stock tanks filled,
No burnt fields, no massive grass fires,
No dry rivers, no dried up springs,
Texas has build over 3000 dams for water storage.

Water means Texans live,
Another year without fear,
Flourishing as God intended,
Texas flush, full of production,
Lack of water stunts Texas growth.

Water gives Texas cities ability to grow,
Texans can then make more impressive advances,
Achieving another tremendous year,
Texans always do their best,
But only, if Texas, has enough water!

God's Chosen Human Angels

Each nurse you meet,
A dedicated care giver,
Takes note of your needs,
Sent to help you,
One of God's chosen human angels.

A most wonderful person,
Practicing a noble vocation,
Fighting for your health,
While under their care,
One of God's chosen human angels.

Always honor them,
For their dedication,
Long hours working,
Against any difficult condition,
One of God's chosen human angels.

They help to solve,
Whatever the problems,
Counseling, encouraging,
Keeping faith with healing care,
One of God's chosen human angels.

They press on as God's human angels,
Ever forward, never back,
Striving against all odds,
With their helping ways,
One of God's chosen human angels.

These such persons,
Are rare indeed,
Always needed,
Lifting spirits of each patient,
One of God's chosen human angels.

When encountered,
They are smiling,
Laughing, always helpful,
Uplifting the ill in every way,
One of God's chosen human angels.

Always hopeful,
With good advice,
Without faulting others,
In any way,
One of God's chosen human angels.

Working hard hours,
Long and difficult,
Even in deepest night,
Caring for God's wounded children,
One of God's chosen human angels.

So God so dear above,
Please give ear,
To my prayer,
This fervent plea,
For God's chosen human angels.

Always stay near,
Those assigned such tasks,
Rare they are indeed,
So needed by all,
Each of God's chosen human angels.

Through Your chosen human angels we see,
Your restoring all,
Your renewing all,
Your creation, the beauty of another day,
Because of God's chosen human angels.

41

Nightmares

When deepest sleep occurs,
Hidden worries may emerge,
With minds deep at rest,
Weird dreams can occur,
Nightmares.

They have no meaning,
Not in reality,
Hidden away in your mind,
Just shadows stirring about,
Nightmares.

Our mind is not focused.
Nor clear,
It is not awake,
Nor aware,
Of nightmares.

Yet worries,
Seem so real,
Senses appear alert,
Situations so real,
Caused by nightmares.

Fret not,
These are hidden worries,
Vivid, scary, out of control,
Happening now,
Unfolding in your nightmares.

In dream time,
Such manifestations,
Or fears, false situations,
Buried deep, unknowingly,
Nightmares seem very real.

All are false situations,
Your mind created,
Its cleaning out trash,
Clearing its memory,
As nightmares unfold.

So fret not over rude awaking,
Caused by nightmares,
As your mind is working,
Clearing itself,
Of nonsensical nightmares stuff.

Nonsense not needed,
Most likely junk,
Things that never happened,
Nor ever will,
Another nightmare cleared.

Because God Himself,
Created self cleaning,
For your mind,
Just for you,
Using your nightmares as His tool.

A Wish

Does a wish ever come true,
Perhaps some do,
Perhaps some not,
Most just dreams,
A wish never to be.

Perhaps, in rare cases,
A good one does become true,
If one wishes,
In the right way,
Carefully.

Might a proper wish,
Be granted,
Backed by good choices,
With honest efforts,
Become true?

I like to think,
Perhaps it does,
As hard work,
Right choices are done,
Such a wish could become true.

A good wish.
Just can come true,
If one's life paths,
Are correctly selected,
At every turn.

With careful navigation,
Proper choices,
Foresight, judgment,
Timing, effort, by you,
Any good wish could become true?

Before making such a wish,
Be as thoughtful as you can,
Choose carefully,
With consideration,
What your wish really does.

Will others be helped,
Blessed, as well as you?
By your wish,
If it comes true?
Be wise, thoughtfully, for a wish can come true!

43

Music

Its sounds come,
In many ways,
Softly, quietly,
But beautifully,
Its music you hear.

Melody clearly building,
Inspiring in quiet beauty,
Soothing, awaking, enabling,
Your deepest feelings,
Its music your hear.

Sounds heard carefully amplified,
As it builds upon itself,
Turning its melodies,
Into heart felt human emotions,
Its music you hear.

Meant to be felt,
Deep in your inner self,
Lifting your soul,
To our God at times,
Its music you hear.

Its words now fully heard,
Delivered by melody to you,
Lifting your life,
To heights of great joy,
Its music you hear.

Perhaps made beautiful,
Blended with perfect choir voices,
Soaring your eternal thoughts,
To the gates of Heaven,
Its music you hear.

It can sooth a person,
With soft quiet melody,
Or destroy a person's tranquility,
With out of tune loud sounds,
Its music you hear.

Various types exist of music,
Extremes from rap to opera,
Conveying human emotions,
Perhaps uplifting, perhaps not,
Its music you hear.

Music should be felt,
When lyrics match its sounds,
Delivering to a listener's ears,
Some lyrical message of life,
Its music you hear.

Examples of same may be,
Worship of God, a religious service,
Or, a loved one remembered,
However lost, in your past years,
Its music you hear.

Music is a language,
Heard often Heaven for sure,
Where glorious melodies are felt,
Deeply, so deeply, in all immortal souls,
Its music you hear.

Each immoral soul,
Upon hearing same,
Joins God's angelic choirs,
Melding together our everlasting eternal souls,
Its the magic of music, for sure, you hear!

44

Serenity

Can you remain calm,
When all others cannot?
Can you stay tranquil,
In extreme circumstances?

Can you stay in control,
As emergency occurs?
If so, you have a wonderful trait,
Serenity.

Can you keep performing,
As others fall apart?
Can you think clearly,
As turmoil occurs?

Can you act correctly,
While under such stress?
If so, you have a tremendous trait,
Serenity.

Can you find solutions,
As limited time expires?
Can you react quickly,
Under extreme pressure?

Can you quickly respond,
When life is at stake?
If so, you have a sought after trait,
Serenity.

Can your courage hold,
In dire situations?
Can your judgment,
Be fair when required?

Can your nerves,
Stay strong and steady?
If so, you have a very rare trait,
Serenity, serenity, serenity, how wonderful to have!

45

Extreme Courage

Extreme courage,
Sought, but a rare quality,
A complete lack of fear,
But needed at times.

Displayed unexpectedly,
As unbelievable bravery,
Perhaps an act of valor in war,
Sacrificing one's life for others.

Such extreme courage,
Rarely seen on display,
Is usually found,
When death itself is sure to be.

Extreme courage appears,
Hidden somewhere deep within,
As one's life may be ending,
In a final courageous act.

Hidden, waiting, unknown,
Extreme courage can be found,
However sparse, its there,
In the depths of your God given soul.

46

Wisdom

Wisdom is a rare,
Much sought human trait,
A base of sound judgment.

No matter what,
It surely grows,
From experience.

Wisdom requires,
Completely knowing oneself,
And knowledge of people.

Certainly wisdom requires,
Deep knowledge of life,
And ability "reading" others.

Wisdom also requires knowledge,
Careful consideration,
For correct decisions.

Especially under stress,
In dire situations,
Without needed facts available.

Wisdom results,
Reaching proper judgments,
In difficult situations.

Wisdom is learning people's character,
Wisdom is grown from experiences,
Wisdom is based on logical reasoning.

Wisdom has been sought,
By many people,
Few ever have much wisdom.

Wisdom was bestowed
On King Solomon,
When God gave him his choice.

Have you wisdom?
If so you are one,
Of the very lucky, lucky, lucky few!

47

Faith

Faith, a most important trait,
A belief you have,
Beyond factual proof.

A feeling very deep within,
A reliance, confident assurance,
Felt by you to be very true.

Many views of God,
Faith in the Creator of all,
May be the greatest example.

Faith in a person,
Absolutely knowing,
Whom you can depend upon.

Faith that your soul,
Lives on after earthly death,
In an eternal life.

Faith,
No matter your religion,
Supports your spiritual side.

Faith is a great gift,
Melds your reasoning,
To your inner spiritual self.

Faith is an extra sense,
Known little about,
Hidden away, but always there.

Faith is in each person,
And it is most important,
In helping to guide one's life.

Faith gives you a more secure path,
Providing confidence, determination,
Found deep in your God created soul.

48

Judgment

Judgment is a decision process,
Based on facts presented,
Never only on feelings,
According to established law.

Judgment delivered,
Sometimes in great haste,
Or perhaps very late,
May be justice in error, or denied.

Thus judgment varies,
It can be in error,
Many times fair,
Sometimes not.

Judgment once made,
Has two faces,
One fair, the other not,
For those being judged.

Either way,
Lives are changed,
Hopefully for the best,
Perhaps not.

Judgment by a judge or jury,
Cannot properly fit,
Every situation foreseen,
Humans are not infallible.

Situations are varied,
We all have seen,
Laws cannot always fit,
All situations thus encountered.

Due to known law,
Many situations are not fully covered,
Space law, maritime law, are examples,
Such areas need additional legal guidelines.

Equal judgment,
For the powerful, for the powerless,
Society should seek, indeed demand,
For judgment and law to be same for all.

Judgment applied fairly,
By all courts of law,
Perhaps it will be someday,
Equal justice for everyone.

After all,
We judge each other,
Every day in every way,
As our time passes on.

49

Choices

Choices are always present,
The act of choosing,
A physical object,
Or just following a thought,
Choices make up your life.

Choices made rapidly,
Or slowly, or skipped,
However badly needed,
Are always there,
Choices will happen, made or not.

When choices are important,
Weight circumstances,
Determine foreseen outcomes,
Good or bad, just remember,
Choices map your path of life.

Choices very important,
Require careful thought,
You gather facts, consider all,
Ask others their opinions,
Cross checking choices helps.

Experiences must be recalled,
Failed choices,
Successful choices,
All remembered, needed now,
Correcting choices improves with years.

Some choices must be hurried,
Perhaps a life is at stake,
Difficult choices to make,
Your good judgment counts,
Hopefully, difficult choices are few.

Most choices are trivial,
What to eat,
When to sleep,
Who to call,
Trivial choices become your habits.

Just remember,
Choices, are always there,
Important or unimportant,
Every day, recognized or not,
Choices make up your life.

50

In Remembrance of a Loved One

O God above us all,
You have called our loved one,
To Your eternal heavenly home,
We must accept Your decision, we know,
We pray to Thee.

O God above us all,
Hear our plea,
We beg of Thee, hear us now,
Give our loved one eternal rest,
We pray to Thee.

O God above us all,
On bend ed knee,
Remember how our loved one fought,
Always brave, to the very end,
We pray to Thee.

O God above us all,
Our loved one cannot suffer now,
Let our loved one's eternal soul rest,
With our others, who went before,
We pray to Thee.

O God above us all,
Treat our loved one gently,
Embrace our loved one carefully,
Our loved one suffered, much, so very much,
We pray to Thee.

O God above us all,
Welcome our loved one,
Keep our loved one in Your care,
We ask once more,
We pray to Thee.

O God above us all,
Dry our tears of grief,
Heal our broken hearts, mend our damaged souls,
We remember, our loved one's life, well lived,
We pray to Thee.

O God above us all,
Tell our loved one of our great loss,
Until in Your heaven, we will be together, for eternity,
Humbly, so gratefully,
We pray to Thee.

The Texas Hornswoggler

Beware, beware,
Of a smooth talking,
Glib tongued,
Oily talking slicker.

Dressed to standout,
To be easily seen,
Quick, so quick,
To invite attention.

With a Texas twang.
In his uttered words,
Each gushing forth,
Enticing to hear.

Mesmerizing as new oil,
Spewing forth from its well.
Trapping you,
With his snake oiled words.

A Texas Hornswoggler,
With no doubt,
Up to his tall tales,
Spouting verbal garbage.

Willing you, entrapping you,
Quickly into schemes,
Blinding good judgment,
Common sense forgotten.

He may be after,
Your money,
Cattle, land, oil,
Property, or even more.

Even worse, far worse,
After your daughter,
Or your sainted wife,
Beware, beware, beware, I say.

Whatever you value,
He always craves,
A Texas Hornswoggler,
He must be.

No morals has he,
In any way,
Never to be trusted,
Avoid, avoid, avoid, his schemes.

Beware, take care,
I say once more, beware,
You have been warned,
Run the other way.

In Texas be on guard,
Watch, watch, watch out,
For the glib tongued,
Oily talking Texas Hornswoggler.

A Taste of Love

You provided me love needed,
You gave me a touch so dear,
You trusted me with all your heart,
You provide a taste of love indeed.

Your trust was wonderfully given,
Your strength melded with mine,
Your energy was near divine,
You provide a taste of love indeed.

You were always there for me,
You listened to my hurts in life,
You encouraged me always to succeed,
You provide a taste of love indeed.

You were my guiding force in life,
You gave always without complaint,
You were always at my side,
You will always be, my eternal taste of love.

53

Awaken Just Once More

My love,
Awaken once more,
From your eternal sleep,
I ask of thee.

As at long last,
I am here near you,
Disturbing your rest,
I know my love.

God Himself,
Brought me at last,
To be with you once again,
I ask of thee.

I am finally here,
To lie again beside you,
My eternal love,
Resting from given tasks.

Remember again,
Our golden days,
Of life, an love,
I ask of thee.

Never forgotten,
I certainly know,
Together once more,
I ask of thee.

Much happiness,
You brought us both,
My life so full of thee,
Remember it, I ask of thee.

So very much love,
Overflowing my life's cup,
Spilling over I swear,
I have never forgotten thee.

Your very touch,
My essence and joy,
Such love,
From thee completed me.

Your presence to me,
A bit of paradise,
On God's earth,
I tell to thee.

I shall thank, you,
In all eternity,
For all you did,
Just for me.

My very soul overflows,
With love untold,
With such nearness,
Once again of thee.

So please awake my love,
From your eternal restful sleep,
And embrace me once more,
Allowing my eternal sleep with you.

I prayed to God above.
That He allows us,
Together once again,
In His eternal care.

I need your love,
Assurance and nearness,
To complete me,
I ask of thee.

I have missed you so,
My wife,
My deepest love,
Together again in eternally.

Until the end of time,
When judgment day arrives,
We shall awaken once more,
Together I ask of thee.

For His final pronouncements,
According to our "Book of Life",
When God Himself will approve,
Of us, together, in His eternal care.

54

A Taste of Heaven

Is a golden sunrise,
Is a clear blue shy,
Is a mountain high,
Is a beautiful moon,
All just a taste of heaven to me.

Is a night full of stars,
Is a redwood tree,
Is a field of blooms,
Is a perfect rose seen,
All just a taste of heaven to me.

Is a loved one near,
Is a child's laughter,
Is joy in living,
Is a lovely smile,
All just a taste of heaven to me.

Is a mate so dear,
Is a hand held tight,
Is a loving hug,
Is a life together,
All the above, just a taste of heaven, for me.

55

What is Life's Meaning?

What does one's life mean to each?
What does each want from living?
What does a single human hope to do?
In short, what does life, living, mean?

What role does the helix of genes mean?
What does your father contribute to same?
What does your mother add with hers?
In short, what does life, living, mean?

What does a child's environment provide?
What does circumstances of birth mean?
What does place and time influence?
In short, what does life, living, mean?

What matters race and place?
What matters height and health?
What matters diet and age?
In short, what does life, living, mean?

What causes a person's character to show?
What intangibles are required to succeed?
What education and traits are so needed?
In short, what does life, living, mean?

What does our Creator plan for each?
What informs us to know?
What are we all to do together, or not?
In short, what does life, living, mean?

What is the brain really reasoning at times?
What is the mind of one doing with same?
What is, and how does, our eternal soul connect with same?
In short, what does life, living, mean?

56

Forgive Me, O Lord God

As I have lived,
Grown older,
Some bit of wisdom,
Has been found.

At last I realize,
What I failed to do,
I think insight occurred,
So I pray, "Forgive me, O Lord God".

Out standing are lessons learned,
But not applied,
Causing grave mistakes,
So I pray, "Forgive me, O Lord God".

So costly,
Not forgotten,
Now so surely aware of same,
So I pray again, "Forgive me, O Lord God".

Opportunities lost in times past,
Now clearly remembered,
Costing my loved ones dearly,
So I pray again, "Forgive me, O Lord God".

Caused by my failure,
My lack of insight,
Obscured by my pride,
So I pray again, "Forgive me, O Lord God".

I did not think clearly,
Because of lack of wisdom,
And a temper not controlled,
So I pray again, "Forgive me, O Lord God".

Now time has moved,
Me down life's path,
And some wisdom grew,
So I pray again, "Forgive me, O Lord God".

Now I clearly see,
In my older years near,
As life begins to close,
So I pray again, "Forgive me, O Lord God".

A bit of wisdom
Earlier in my years here,
Should I have had,
So I pray again, "Forgive me, O Lord God".

Finally, so late now, finally I see,
I ask for Your forgiveness,
On bend ed knee, humbly,
Once more to Thee, "Forgive me, O Lord God".

Eternal Time

What is time?
Where does it begin?
Where does it end?
What does it mean?

Who started time?
Who ends time?
Who measures time?
Who changes time?

When does time slow?
When does time speed up?
When is time past?
What is time present?

Is time constant?
Is time a variable?
Is time a flow?
Is time eternal?

Is time meaningful,
In a short life lived,
In a long life lived?
Is eternal time meant to be for you?

Circumstances and Time

Circumstances, conditions found,
Circumstances, situations present,
Circumstances, cannot be perfect,
Circumstances, often unexpected.

Circumstances, always changing,
Circumstances, awareness required,
Circumstances, requiring decisions,
Circumstances, needing actions done.

Circumstances, may be good,
Circumstances, may be bad,
Circumstances, can be dealt with,
Circumstances, always change with time.

Time, moves forward,
Time, most valuable,
Time, never enough,
Time, varies life.

Time, brings changes,
Time, cannot repeat,
Time, brings circumstances,
Time, always changes with circumstances.

59

Forgive My Sins

Forgive, my sins committed,
Forgive, my tasks left undone,
Forgive, my mistakes in this life,
O Lord above, all I give to You.

Are sins, tasks left undone?
Are sins, mistakes made in my life?
If they are, as they may well be,
O Lord above, please forgive me.

My sins, very deep,
My sins, hard to forget,
My sins, easily remembered,
O Lord above, please forgive me.

My sins, in the past,
My sins, dreamed about,
My sins, part of me,
O Lord above, I must let it be.

My sins, never to change,
My sins, vivid still,
My sins, in me still,
O Lord above, help me put such sins aside.

After all, You went to the cross,
After all, You took sins from me,
After all, You died for all my sins,
O Lord above, my soul thanks You, my soul thanks You!

A Father's View of Each Daughter

A father looks at each daughter,
Always carefully,
Always lovingly,
Always gratefully,
And always thankfully.

Each daughter a great gift,
Each is his pride and joy,
A great treasure of his,
Cared for a period of years,
And always thankfully.

Each daughter is love itself,
A potential new family to be,
Making daughters very special,
Carrying forward promised life itself,
And always thankfully.

When each daughter becomes a woman grown,
Each carries a fathers special pride,
His words are full of joy for her,
His deep love is always hers,
As he gives her carefully, to her chosen man.

He always remembers, always, "My daughter, mine1

61

But Found Again

As years pass,
Former friends,
Acquaintances,
Family members are lost.

They are buried,
Vanished,
Forgotten,
Within the shadows of time.

Once loved,
Needed,
Treasured,
Making life so worthy.

As decades pass by,
Life's changes require,
Such memories be stored away,
In fade less time, far away.

Not lost forever,
Hopefully later to recall,
The good remembered,
The bad forgotten.

Time itself can heal,
Faults,
Disagreements,
Conflicts that occurred.

One only remembering the good,
Erasing the differences,
Recalled again the best,
From fading times so long ago.

Remembrances known of others,
Filling your life once more,
With those thought lost,
But found again.

62

Your Touch

You reach out,
Quietly,
Carefully,
Just to touch me.

At such times,
My heart slows,
Knowing once more,
You again so near.

My spirit soars,
Such a touch,
Caresses my soul,
Deeply within me.

Once more to feel,
Your gentle touch,
Conveying such love,
Given me.

What a lifetime,
Together we had,
Such wondrous joys,
I know once more.

Such a touch,
From heaven,
From thee,
To me.

63

I Believe

I believe in,
An Eternal God,
Who gave me,
My everlasting soul.

I believe that,
Same Eternal God,
Setting me on my path,
Meant me to be bold.

I believe that,
God always provides,
And He created goals,
For me to reach.

I believe that,
God's everlasting strength,
Which is always near,
Strengthens me as needed.

I believe that,
God gave freedom,
And life,
Not only to me, but to all.

I believe that,
God wants all of us,
To learn His love,
As our life's unfold.

I believe that,
Our eternal God,
Upon finishing our paths,
Welcomes back, our everlasting souls.

64

The Texas Bluebonnets

A field of Texas bluebonnets,
Seen early in the spring,
Radiates to all,
Breathtaking beauty.

They sooth your soul,
Brighten your spirit,
Reassuring all, part of heaven,
Is here once more.

Another reminder,
From God,
For all to see,
Texas is blessed.

Blue as the azure Texas sky,
Fulfilling once more,
Texas promises,
Creator made.

Renewal,
Another beginning,
Life's march of time,
Ever onward.

Forward life moves,
A starting over,
Promised each spring,
In such a beautiful way

Each petal perfect,
Forming a wild flower,
So very inspiring,
For all to see.

Colored in deep blue,
Bluer than any sky,
Found each spring,
Only in Texas.

Renewing life's beauty,
Texas bluebonnets proclaim,
A piece of heaven itself,
Is there for all to see.

Each bluebonnet field,
With its heavenly blue,
A glorious sight to see,
Renewed once more.

Our forefathers saw,
Their awsome beauty,
Understood fully,
Our Creator sent same.

Reminding all Texans,
That a bit of heaven,
Belongs in Texas too,
Always in Texas, always.

65

The Texas Whip-poor-will's Nocturnal Call

During early Texas Spring,
Just as the sun ceases,
Another shining day,
Listen carefully, very carefully.

Dring this twilight time,
As evening begins,
A bird's beautiful call may be heard,
Sounding sorrowful, very mournful.

Calling for its lost companion,
Very quietly, softfully,
Such a beautiful melody,
Of a soul's longing needs.

Its beauty of sound,
Carries its mournful plea,
One of very deep need,
Quietly, quietly heard.

Carried by the twilight air,
As nature stands still,
Being still, very still,
To hear the call of sorrowful plea.

Only heard at twilight,
Early in a Texas Spring,
Just at close of day,
A small echoed sound.

Calling "Whip-poor-will",
Again, "Whip-poor-will",
Carrying its lonely meaning,
Deep into your heart

Quite in volume,
So hard to hear,
Even your heart beats,
Must wait a bit.

Extremely low in volume,
It asks within its cry,
"Where-are-you?",
"Where-are-you?".

It repeats again, an again,
Saying in its call,
"I-need-you",
"I-need-you".

Calling again, an again,
"Come-to- me"
"Come-to-me",
Over and over.

As you strain to hear,
Such lonely quiet sounds,
All of nature seems to stop,
To hear the call as well.

All life itself understands,
The Whip-poor-will's need,
Even early night stars seem to wait,
On starting their twinkling lights.

The Whip-poor-will's call is hear again,
Its call now says,
"My-soul-hurts",
"My-soul- hurts".

Calling again, and again,
"I-am-here",
"I-am-here",
Such meaning now clear to you.

In a most beautiful way,
A last call, a lonesome cry,
Barely heard, low but clear,
Its twilight call now may end.

When you hear a soft reply,
"Our-love-forever",
"Our-love-forever",
So very clear, so very near.

Then followed now,
By a quietly answering call,
"My-soul-knows",
"My-soul- knows".

A closing call, now in response,
"I-miss-you",
"I-miss-you",
Having filled finally its poor soul's needs.

66

A Father's Prayer

Almighty God,
I humbly offer,
My soul felt gratitude.

For giving unto me,
The most treasured gift,
Which I can receive.

The gift of being a father,
Helping to create,
Another human being.

Brought to completion,
Within my wife's loving care,
You Lord, providing the soul.

Almighty God,
No higher privilege, gift,
Wonder, can be bestowed.

Life for me,
Would be empty,
Without a child, I know.

Continuing humanity's chain,
By those who came before,
Now once more.

Never let me forget,
My duty to each child,
Given to me for care.

Such duty shall last,
All my life on this earth,
Allowed to me.

Help me do my best,
For each, to be provider,
Protector, adviser, mentor.

Nourishing each child's needs,
Aiding every step of growth,
Spiritual, mental, emotional, physical.

Lord God accept,
My soul felt gratitude,
Allowing me such a high previlidge.

I shall mightly strive,
To be the father,
You want me to be.

Loving each child,
Joyfully, thankfully,
Entrusted into my care.

Remembering in my soul,
Because of Thee,
I hear a wonderful sound, "Dad...., Father...., Pop,...."

67

The Texas Heat

During any summer day,
Under a clear Texas sky,
Precautions are needed,
Be fully aware.

Rattlesnakes seek shade,
Cattle, horses, hide in the breaks,
Only buzzards might fly,
Insects escape under ground.

Because intense killing heat,
Generated beyond belief,
Comes to all, from a hot ball,
High in the Texas sky.

Texas people survive,
Knowing what to do,
And what not to do,
In arid, punishing, furnace heat.

A ten gallon cowboy hat,
Or a Mexican sombrero helps,
Providing shade for your head,
Keeping brain, body, a bit cooler.

Large quantities of cool water,
Lots of shade from trees,
Better yet, retreat inside,
During the furnace heat of day.

Staying alive means life slows,
During fierce Texas summer days,
Shade, water, light dress,
Some still use the siesta for rest.

Starting your day early helps,
Outside tasks are done,
Before the sun rises high,
Midday siesta is then won.

But all take heart,
Even in depths of summer,
As night begins to fall,
Life survives from Texas heat.

68

A Mother's Prayer

Almighty God,
I humbly offer,
My soul felt gratitude.

For giving unto me,
The most treasured gift,
Which I can receive.

The gift of being a mother,
Helping to create,
Another human being.

Brought to completion in my womb,
With loving care,
With You, Lord, providing the soul.

Almighty God,
No higher privilege, gift,
Wonder, can be bestowed.

Life for me,
Would be empty,
Without each child given to me.

Continuing humanity's chain,
Formed by those,
Who came before.

Never let me forget,
My duty to each child,
Given to me, Almighty God.

Duty of motherhood lasts,
Through my life on this earth,
Allowed by You.

Help me do my best,
For each child, to be loving,
Caring, adviseing, helpful.

Nourishing each child's needs,
Aiding every step of growth,
Spiritual, mental, emotional, physical.

So Lord God accept,
My soul felt gratitude,
For such an opportunity.

I shall strive,
To be the mother,
You want me to be.

Loving each child,
Given to me, joyfully,
Gratefully, thankfully

Remembering in my soul,
Because of Thee,
I hear such sounds as, "Mom..., Mother.., Mama..."

69

Just Me

Into this world I came,
With nothing,
Attached, nor brought,
Just me.

Completely naked,
Unclothed, bare,
Crying, scared,
As you can be.

Only equipped with,
A body and mind,
By my parents,
And soul by God was I

Totally dependent,
Upon all others,
For years yet to come,
This was me.

No title of royalty,
Entitlements none,
Nothing to offer,
That was me.

As years pasted,
My body, mind, and soul,
Grew with each year,
Having experiences anew.

Childhood flew by,
Fast as allowed,
To be fully remembered,
By just me.

An education occured,
In every aspect of life,
On ever subject required,
Daily occurred, as life unfolded for me.

Some I liked,
Some I failed,
Passing into a life,
Full of wonder, great joy, and suffering too.

I was told that's life,
Keep going,
Duty, honor,
Country, responsibility, is for me.

So never I stopped,
Quit, or pause to long,
Just always doing,
What must be done by me.

Moving forward,
Goals to met, tasks to finished,
Go on, never slipping back,
Or failure will win.

As my life progressed,
I have not gathered titles,
Awards, fame, nor fortune,
For me.

But, I have helped,
All I could,
When I could,
As duty, honor, country called.

God's guiding hand,
Has been present,
When needed,
Sought by me.

So when my call comes,
To leave this wonderful life,
Joining those who loved me so,
I can gladly go.

Perhaps Poetry

Perhaps poetry,
Is the language,
Used by God's angels.

Spoken by angels,
In a manner,
We cannot hear.

In a soft unheard,
Meaningful manner,
Not meant for us.

A language of caring,
Duty, spirtual meaning,
With love for all.

Perhaps our ears,
Are not tuned to hear,
Such poetic conversations.

Unless God Himself,
Has a special message,
For His people to hear.

Then, and only then,
At the moment chosen,
We are allowed to do so.

With poetic clarity,
His angelic messengers,
Deliver same.

Perhaps,
Living in our mortal shells,
We are not in His eternal time.

It is best that God's angels,
Deliver His messages,
In such a fashion.

For it is surely true,
Such beings are always busy,
With Heaven's work.

Because we at times,
Seem not to hear,
His poetic messages sent.

Perhaps such messages,
Are so beautiful in form,
Content and promise.

Since our Great Creator,
Of our eternal souls,
Cares for each of us.

Or since the angelic delivery,
Of such utterances is so above,
Our level of understanding.

We do not hear,
Poetic deliverance,
Such meanings by our ears.

Perhaps a fortunate few,
Here on this earth of ours,
Have, on rare occasion.

Thus, His messages,
Have been delivered, understood,
Repeated for all to hear.

Placing upon everyone,
His messages of total, complete,
Love for all under His care.

Behold and See

Don't you,
Care at all?
All of you,
Passing thru this life?

Look I say,
Just look again.
Open your eyes,
Behold and see!

Don't each of you,
Care at all?
Knowing of Jesus,
Dying for you?

Look again,
Think once more,
Open your mind, your soul,
To understand at last.

Don't you,
Care at all?
As you walk down,
Your life's path.

Look, think, feel,
With your soul,
Knowing what He did,
Behold, understand.

Don't you,
Care at all?
As your life,
Now flows past.

Accept what He said,
What He did for all,
Your eternal self knows,
Behold and see!

Don't you,
Care at all?
He offers you,
Eternal glorious life!

Now, on the cross,
He takes your sins,
Upon Himself,
Accept, behold, and see!

With Pride, Take Care

Take care,
Controlling your pride,
It can turn "on a dime",
Harming you or others.

Quietly, pride can apear,
Like a thief in the night,
Silently, unexpectedly,
Striking you down.

Damage pride inflicts,
Which may not be felt at once,
But later appears its hurt,
Never to be undone.

It might take years,
To recognize prides effects,
Remaining under cover,
Time long past for any repair.

Harm by your pride,
Cannot be rectified,
Hurt to you and others,
Cannot never be removed.

Once done,
It's done,
Never forgotten by the giver,
Nor forgiven by the receiver.

Hubris, nay pride,
Must be guarded against,
As it is like an echo,
Sounded between mountains.

Reflected again, again,
Again, and again,
One should take great care,
Your use of your pride.

Love, Given to Me

Love should be gentle,
Just a light touch,
Embodied, carried,
By a soul to match.

Gental, softly,
Like a light falling rain,
Giving life itself,
To one's garden of life.

Love must be given,
Freely, never demanded,
As a live spiritual thing,
Of unmeasureable value.

Like gentle rays of sunlight,
Shining brightly,
Growing always,
In one's life.

Love is expression,
Found in God's gift of living,
Carried between each of us,
Nourishing ment for eternal souls.

Binding together all,
Measuring,
One's eternal thanks,
In our garden of life.

Love is a bit of heaven,
Given at birth,
Sealed into each,
For later giving to others.

To be freely seen,
In times of need,
Shinning forth,
Growing in our garden of life.

Love is what you,
Give others,
Watering life to grow,
Bringing beauty to the soul.

74

With a Glance Back

On this day,
Remembering,
Remembering all of your beauty,
Radiance, and sheer love.

Love so freely given,
Without a thought,
To be remembered,
When glancing in time.

On this day,
Just a glance gives me vision,
Seeing you once again.
Your grace, beauty, spirit, and soul.

You are remembered,
Once more,
By family, friends, loved ones,
Of a life well lived.

On this day,
But a glance forward also made,
Seeing God's gift to you,
Of life forever, with boundless love.

To be seen by all,
Who loved you so,
Just glances, back, and forward,
Seeing you again, always, always, always....

Never Forgetting, Always Remembering

As the years melt,
Into the vast abyss,
Of endless past times.

I remember you,
Young and beautiful,
Vibrant, radiant with life.

A beauty in body, soul,
Spirit, and mind,
A wonder to all.

And I remember,
Never forgetting,
Remembering your love.

When each child came,
Life anew, celebration,
Happiness unbounded.

I remember you,
Like sunshine showering down,
Radiating love.

More than a beauty,
In body and soul,
A woman in all her glory.

And I remember,
Never forgetting,
Remembering all now.

As each child grew,
Passing from infant to youth,
To be a mature adult.

I remember you,
Helping, loving,
Listening, advising each.

A saint, full of sacrifice,
A protector, full of fury,
But always full of love.

And I remember,
Never forgetting,
Always remembering.

Now the day seems to be done,
The quest almost fulfilled,
As each as gone their way.

I remember you,
Still seeking to help others,
Making a difference, contributing to all.

A mature beauty, radiating grace,
Charm, wit, and boundless love,
A wonder to all.

And I remember,
Never forgetting,
Always remembering.

Now all seems to be done,
The vast abyss of endless time,
Moves on, moves on, again.

I remember you,
My mate, completing my soul,
Giving my existence meaning.

Wise counselor, stout pillar,
An unending wall of support,
Through it all.

And I remember,
Never forgetting,
Always remembering, remembering, remembering.

A Whisper to Remember

Last night as I slept,
I heard a whisper,
From God Himself.

Laura is fine here,
With loved ones,
All in heaven's embrace.

She walks again,
No aid required,
Strong and straight.

Never will she fall,
Hurt, feel earthly pains,
Never again.

Guardian angels,
Assigned toher care,
Shall always be near.

Watchful, protecting,
Advising, ensuring her,
Of your continuing love.

No harm be allowed,
In entire eternity,
To cross her path.

Laura has paid the price,
Not even owed,
For such eternal bliss.

All her fears, concerns,
Hurts have been banished,
By God's direct order.

No more examinations,
Medications, treatments,
Hospitals, surgeries needed.

Laura's heavenly body,
Made from her pure soul,
Is perfect as can be.

Her enduring soul,
Courage, determination,
Are not lost, but always here.

She is fine once more,
She will wait for you,
When the Angel of Death brings you here.

Bringing you back to her,
God's whisper gently said,
Quietly in my mind.

Reasuring me once more,
Of Laura's continued love,
For me, our children, and family.

All still on God's wonderful earth,
As God's whisper,
Softly faded into the night.

I then heard a familiar voice say,
Live well, live strong, fear not,
Embrace life, God's precious gift.

Remembering my love for you,
Until we eternaly embrace in heaven,
I am your Laura.

An Instrument of God's Devine Plan

Lord, make me,
An instrument,
Of Your divine vision.

Give me direction,
Wit, and needed drive,
Helping Your divine plan.

So all following,
After me,
Shall strive as well.

Reaching toward,
Your divine goals,
Set for our humble souls.

Lord, forgive us all,
For not understanding,
Your insights given in holy texts.

Written by Your gifted prophets,
Many ages ago,
To instruct us on what to do.

Misunderstood,
Not followed,
Or wrongley used.

Christ Himself,
We even crucified,
Your only earthly Son.

Lord, give me drive,
Energy, health, tools needed,
To help achieve Your vision.

Do not allow me to fail,
Stumble, falter,
Before I too contribute.

I pray to Thee,
For direction,
Your guidence needed.

Forgive me,
When I digress,
Keep me on the right path.

78

My Guardian Angels

Upon our birth,
God assign's one,
Or, on rare occasions,
Two Guardian Angels.

Whose duties are,
To guard you,
Soul and all,
As you live your life here.

I know,
I am amoung the few,
My need was foreseen,
God did send two just for me.

They have been near,
Keeping close watch,
Protecting, warrning, watching,
Hidden beyond my given sight.

Drastic, even fatal harm,
Has past me by,
In every case I survived,
Because of my Guardian Angels.

Carrying swords an shields,
Issued by Heavens armory,
Used protecting my soul,
From harm I do not see.

These blessed swords an shields,
Can fracture any evil,
Placed in my path of life,
To do harm to me.

My guardian angels names,
Will never be known,
To me in this life,
Or anyone else on this earth.

Nor mostly likely,
Never to even my soul,
My spirit,
Nor eternal mind.

Until that moment,
I am called to join,
My beloved wife,
An all who went before.

To live the eternal life,
With all I loved here on earth,
Promised by Jesus Christ Himself,
Who loves, cherishes us all.

My "Book of Life" will be read,
Entering God's eternal domain,
Aloud, checked, approved,
Thus assuring my entry.

As my Heavenly crown,
Hard earned from a life lived here,
Helping to fulfill God's plans,
Is awarded to me.

I shall then turn,
To my two Guardian Angels,
Giving them my eternal thanks,
Your job was well done, well done indeed

79

A US Marine's Prayer

Lord God, I beseech Thee,
Listen to my prayer,
I am but a humble servant of Yours.

I must now use weapons of war,
Upon those who bring nothing,
But fear, destruction, and death.

Make me yours, I ask of Thee,
Give me strength and courage,
To assure my loved ones their safety, I pray.

Providing all I am sworn to protect,
That fear, harm, hurt, even death,
I shall turn away from them.

Give me a unswerving will,
Inflicting destruction fast,
Furious, decisive, upon all my foes.

That such foes shall fear me,
Fall before me, destroyed,
By all such forces I can use.

Future foes shall then quake,
At the thought of facing Marines,
In any time and any place.

Never allowing harm,
To the innocents, noncombatants,
My loved ones I aim to protect.

I will always be faithful,
Lord God to You,
Marine Corps, my country, and family.

I must fight for what's right,
Be at my side, day and night,
As the battle rages about.

Keep me brave, true, never afraid,
Using my warrior skills for Your goals,
Bless me, with Your eternal grace, I pray to You.

A Warriors Lament

Dear God I pray,
Stand on my side,
Never on my foe's side.

My foes spreads fear, terrior, death,
I pray most earnestly to You,
Move away from my foes to me.

Then stand by,
To witness our fight,
Victory or death, Isay.

I shall do all in my power,
To obliterate such evil ones,
From this earth of Yours.

Upon my victory hard won,
I shall show all mercies,
Following Your given rules.

To the vanquished foes,
Justice done according to law,
For all evil done by them.

Knowing then,
An only then,
Your approval shall be mine.

Once more peace,
Security, life, duty, even honor,
Will again be for all, with their safety assured.

81

Hidden Memories

Very deep in my soul,
I keep hidden,
My memories of you.

Only I, and I alone,
Know how wonderful,
Life was with you by my side.

With careful care, of such memories,
Treading with the lightest step,
I dare enter there.

Such hidden memories,
Sir my deepest emotions,
I have remembered of you.

The dearest one,
In my entire life was,
Has been, always, will be you.

Such soul stored,
Hidden memories,
Must be treated with a tender touch.

Carefully unwrapped,
From a life remembered,
A time an place of greatest joy.

Happiness remembered,
Of you, my dearest love,
Again to be savored once more.

To quickly, the wonderful taste of our love,
Hidden memories, must be moved,
Back to their time.

They are again safely put away,
Deep into my soul's hidden,
Storage place.

Never to be shared with others,
Only between you an me,
And God.

As now you are in,
Our Saviours promised heaven,
Forever under God's eternal watch.

I know your soul, spirit,
Your meaningful self,
Are totally secure under heaven's watch.

As are my hidden memories,
Our glorious moments, our life,
Affection, gratitude, of living together.

Until we are united again,
Within God's glorious grace,
Together for eternity.

Such wonderful, shinning,
Hidden memories,
Keep me living in life's fullest embrace.

82

A Morning Greeting

May the radiance,
Of every new day,
Shine brightly upon you.

Filling ever moment,
From your rising,
With happy thoughts.

With all of God's creation,
At peace during your slumber,
Refreshing you once more.

Your body, mind, emotions,
Even your soul,
Looking forward to a new day.

May your new day,
Overflow with gladness,
Having blessings beyond measure.

Spilling life's joys,
Upon all throughout,
Spreading happiness about.

May such happiness,
Be always yours,
Sharing with others another day.

And may every morning,
You greet every new day,
The same in every way.

83

Bless Our Nation, God

God,
We trust,
In Your divine mercy.

For only You,
Can lift misery,
From our land.

Thou are almighty,
Above all found,
Our creator, our God.

You who created all,
We humbly ask,
Bestow Your grace and blessings.

Divine One,
Bless Your meek, Your poor,
In this nation of ours.

Forgive all of us,
Sinners all,
Lift Your anger from us.

For we are nut mortals,
Mere humans,
Weak people in all ways.

So often wrong in deed,
Judgement, actions,
We ask, have mercy upon us.

Heal the sick,
Mend the lame,
Protect the weak.

Please God,
Keep famine, war, illness,
At bay.

Spread thy kindness,
Shine they grace,
Forgive us our sins.

Hear our lamentations,
Have mercy upon us,
For thou are the Mighty One.

We lift our voices,
Singing praises,
Singing praises to you.

Our life, soul,
Eternal existence,
Is placed in Your hands.

We humbly request once more,
Bless our nation, efforts, souls,
We pray again, an again, an again.

84

Time Moves

As time moves forward,
Once more another loved one leaves,
God, I beg Thee,
Tell us how to walk back time.

God, I beg Thee,
Most Magnificent One,
Tell us how to do so,
Cannot You control time?

Cannot time itself,
Be changed, selected,
Just tell us how,
God, please do so.

As time moves,
Only forward it seems,
Another loved one departs us,
To be losted as time moves.

God, Master of All,
What is time, where is time,
Why is time our master,
Is their negative time as well?

Cannot time be recalled,
Brought back,
Made to obey, controlled,
Changed by willing it so?

God stoped time once,
Why not divide time,
Into two parallels,
Or even many, for us mortals?

As time moves forward,
Another loved one is taken,
A life vanishes before us,
I bow on bended knee.

Before Thee,
Dear God I acknowledge,
You are controller of everthing,
Even our movements in time.

Only bend,
Not break,
Times remembered by me,
Of all my beloved ones.

For time means nothing,
I think, to You,
The Timeless One in eternity,
But to me, its an empting hourglass.

Because time moves forward,
Only forward here,
Separaing loved ones,
Again, an again, an again!

Only I cannot stop, break, bend, control,
Nor change time at all,
Just have sweet memories,
Of times gone by.

Only time itself started,
By You, Supreme Creator of eternity,
Only You remember why it moves so,
And why must it be so.

But time for each of us here,
Will surely end,
Bringing together once again,
Loved ones, in a timeless embrace, I pray.

For Our Sailor

May God's hand,
Be ever present,
Protecting you.

May His grace,
Wherever you navigate,
Shine upon you.

Keeping your sails full,
In His vast seas,
On a proper course.

May God remember,
To keep watch,
Over all on your ship.

His seas are large,
Rough, deep,
Fraught with dangers.

May He help you,
Past all harms,
Found on His oceans.

May He send,
Sunshine, gentle rains,
Soft blowing breezes.

May His skies be clear,
Guiding your ship,
Nights full of stars.

May He help you as needed,
Keeping your and crew allert,
Seas calm, all shipshape.

Leading you, guiding you,
To all your ports of call, finally,
Once again home, save, completely safe.

86

A First Kiss

I hesitated,
Quaking with fear,
Indeed, faint hearted too.

Dare I ask, beg,
Just a favor,
Bestowed from you.

Upon me.
A humble young man,
With a simple soul.

Asking from one,
Having such grace, charm,
Radiant beauty.

From such a one as you,
Even a Greek God,
Would dare not to do.

But I must, beg, plead,
Just a brief kiss,
Be bestowed by you.

For such emotion,
Such transformation,
Such wonder, such feeling.

Will be transmitted,
Into the depths of my body,
Even to my mind, and soul.

Leave me not,
Knowing of you,
Such a first kiss.

Often remembered,
It is sure to be,
In my later years.

Never to be forgotten,
My first kiss,
Given by you, to me.

87

My Wife

A song of love,
Is always heard,
In her voice.

My ear strains,
For her each sparkling,
Uttered sound.

To think I was,
Her choice from many,
Many suitors humbles me.

Nay, to hope,
Even pray,
It may always be so.

O God, Most Merciful,
Thank You,
For giving me ears to hear.

I hear in my dreams,
Her voice once more,
Listening to her very soul.

For she means to me,
Like the heavens wonders,
As Your stars give light.

Her sparkling voice I hear again an again,
Its music to my being's very core,
Need I say more.

88

Missing You

How much,
I miss you,
Cannot be determine,
Never can it be measured.

For it is the same,
As trying to count,
All of God's stars,
In this wonderous universe.

Or numbering,
Every grain of sand,
Found on every beach,
Of every ocean on this earth.

Even more than remembering,
All the wishes ever made,
By lonely, forgotten, lost people,
That have ever lived.

Missing your very presence,
Not here by my side,
Never to be again here, I know,
Cuts into the depths of my soul.

Pouring out its contents,
Upon the sands of our time,
Each grain of together, lost forever,
This I now know.

Never to be recovered,
My soul cannot be healed,
Be fulfilled, completed, until we,
Are together again, my only love.

Both under our Creator's,
Eternal watchful care,
Never again to be apart,
Forming our completed self, in His eternity.

Never Alone

My eyes are raised,
To the heavens so high,
And I felt fear,
God himself was near,
I became very afraid.

O God, why am I alone,
Must I always be so,
What have I done,
Deserving this solitude,
I ask the Creator of all.

I waited for His answer,
As darkness grew,
With my eyes raised,
To the heavens above,
Waiting, waiting to hear.

Then I heard it,
His night bird singing,
A song praising God,
Such a wonderous sound,
Surronding all of me.

With every single,
Glorious note heard,
My world stood still,
And then I knew,
What that answer meant.

My soul is to be filled,
I am not alone,
God's grace is given to me,
Never alone to be,
With such a song in the air.

My memory stirred,
Blessings have occured,
For I have memories of you,
The one God Himself,
Sent to share life with me.

Now my solitude is gone,
Never to harm me ever again,
God's wonderful gift of life,
On this earth we have lived,
I am assured we will be together again.

Beauty

Not only is beauty,
Seen "In the Eye of the Beholder",
But its recognition is found,
In the soul of the beholder.

Thus beauty in living,
Enables one's spirtual eye,
To see all true beauty,
In many different ways.

Life itself is framed,
In a mother's love,
In a father's devotion,
In nature's wonders.

Beauty is found,
Seeing a glorious mountain pass,
Climing the highest peaks,
Towering so high above.

Snow covered,
Cloud hidden,
Magnificent they are,
Rreaching to the sky.

Beauty again appears,
Upon a ocean gaze,
Toward a far distant horizon,
Endless it seems.

Showing the earth's curve,
Displaying the mystery of gravity,
A great unseen force,
Shapping, controlling, all of us.

Putting sailors on the ocean,
Deeply thinking about life,
Powerfully felt,
As ocean waves roll along.

Rocking so gently,
Their ship about,
On the endless sea,
The beauty of life itself.

Beauty appears,
In a mother's concern,
Her love and care,
Of her children dear.

Love always there,
Never lost,
Or spent carelessly,
Available as needed in her life.

Always to help,
Aid, comforting,
Soothing, reassuring,
Beauty with love abundant.

Beauty occurs,
Aound the clock of time,
Unexpected, but always,
Welcomed just the same.

It is in a grandchild's smile,
Laughter, happiness,
Another life continuing,
In a most wonderful way.

Adding flavor to life,
Improving its taste,
Smell, and feel,
To all with loving care.

Beauty is present,
In a clear night's sky,
Where our Creator placed stars,
Countless, gloriously shining to see.

Beauty placed for ever,
Writing a message,
For all to see,
Looking deep into infinity.

Never to be matched,
A beautiful breathless eternal display,
Of God's never-ending reflections,
For all living souls to see.

91

Duty

Duty is doing,
What is expected,
By one to do.

No matter what,
Circumstances, cost,
Or dangers may be.

Regardless,
If life itself lost,
Duty accomplished must be.

Duty is a sacrifice,
And cannot be bought,
Even done at times without thought.

Never delayed,
But always done,
Regardless of risk or loss.

Duty is finished,
Whenever the doer.
Has carried same out.

No fanfare,
No reward,
Nothing paid.

Help may or may not,
Be contributed,
By others.

However its done,
It never can be bought,
Nor sold at all.

So duty is a must,
By one or many,
With no reward or credit asked.

Because it comes,
In one's life,
At unexpected times.

Once duty is done,
Recognized, completed,
It is done, life moves on.

Honor

Honor is a quality,
Each individual,
Has deep within.

Upon swearing same,
Carefully given,
It is a sacred oath.

We must rely,
Upon it once done,
Upheld, solid, never broken.

If it is not,
An individaul's actions, words,
Are but nonsense, a trust broken.

Honor ensures duty,
A military member's guide,
Performing expected actions.

Because brothers in arms,
Country, family, freedom,
Can be at lost without honor.

Honor once stated,
By an oath given,
One's very life is comitted.

Because all civilization,
Depends upon it,
Keeping life stable, for all.

Honor when given,
Is a solid promise,
Never to be broken.

Solid, sound, firm,
A foundation,
We build life around.

Honor is needed, to be understood,
Between husband an wife,
Children, parents, family and all.

It is worth more,
Than gold, precious gems,
Or vast treasures.

Never bought, traded, lost,
But always within reach,
Deep within each person.

Honor is given,
To all at birth,
For this life's use.

To be spent carefully,
As occasion requires,
Later in life,

Never wasted,
Nor thrown about,
Even as many may do.

Honor must be,
Given with care, thought,
Treated as a priceless gift above all.

Country

My country is founded,
Bought for me in blood,
Upon great guarantees.

Such as sacrifice, courage,
Determination, a willingness,
Never ever to quit.

Bold actions carried out,
In the face of odds,
Thought insurmountable.

By men and women,
Who never gave up,
Determined to win.

Win they did,
Founding patriots,
Gave me freedom.

Liberty, equality,
Religious choice,
Even pursuit of happiness.

Life without fear,
Choices I make myself,
Government peopled by choice.

Not me serving government,
Living at a government's pleasure,
Instead, it serves me.

My country serves my interests,
Guaranteed by a Bill of Rights,
With a written Constitution.

Including a representative legislature,
Members I can freely choose,
Call upon, and direct.

Once elected, once in office,
Members can be removed,
Held accountable, dismissed from power.

This is my country,
Were justice prevails, balanced,
By citizen juries required.

My country is a freedom beacon,
For the entire world,
Strong, fighting for right.

Full of people,
Loving life's freedoms,
Written down, guaranteed for all.

Protected,
By courts of law,
Upon which life, family, my welfare depends.

Ensured by a free, open,
Responsive, courageous,
Determined people for freedom.

My country, our country,
Long may it endure, freedom for all,
God bless the United States of America!

94

Questions on Life

Great Creator,
God of All,
I humbly ask of Thee.
Please answer some questions.

They follow now,
My Lord and Savior,
In a stated brief,
Short form of mine.

Some good people,
Wonderful as they are,
Have to suffer so greatly,
In their life on this earth, why?

Some bad people,
Terrible in many ways,
Are allowed to harm others,
Harming them at will, why?

Many dependent children,
Innocents, helpless,
Are deprived of basic necessities,
Food, shelter, love, why?

Murder, robbery,
Theft, rape, torture,
An other depraved acts,
Never seem to end, why?

Great trust placed,
In people in high, lofty,
Powerful, important positions,
Is often deliberately misused, why

Many politicians, lawyers, judges,
Seem to lie, cheat, steal,
Knowingly from society,
Seemly easily done, why?

As an individual,
Each person travels through,
Their life's given journey,
At times unknown to them, why?

Very few can every see,
Clearly obstacles ahead,
Dangers, harms, hurts,
Unknowns of every type, why?

Such obstacles must be,
Avoided, gone around,
Or solved with effort,
Else great hurt occurs.

Such tests, trials,
Should be remembered,
Taught to loved ones,
Is that there purpose?

Is life meant to beat some,
Those who cannot cope,
Pain inflicted, hurt felt,
Even if they cannot help them selves?

Or, if a person suffers,
Then copes with such,
Are the lessons learned,
Passed on, or repeated again?

Does strengthening of spirit result,
Causing a more mature eternal soul,
In those as a result,
This I would like to know.

Building a better soul,
For each person in every way,
Preparing each for our eventual,
Heavenly acceptance by You.

These questions on life,
An many, so many more,
Cannot be answered,
By simple men alone I know.

Much greater minds,
Famous philosophers,
Theologians, prophets,
Others have tried and failed.

Always they fail,
No real answers come forth,
To my simple questions,
I know, but why?

So Great Creator,
Our God of All,
Why, just why, is our life,
Burdened so?

95

Some Answers, Maybe?

Answers are wanted,
To life's simple questions,
But remain unanswered,
Here on this earth.

However, when for each,
The Angel of Death comes,
Touching one's shoulder,
To gathering in another soul.

Carrying it from this life,
To the Gates of Heaven,
For entry into eternity,
Met by the gatekeeper, Saint Peter.

Each Book of Life,
Shall be opened,
Read, worth determined,
Then weighted on God's scales.

Answers shall come forth,
In full measure to each,
All questions each have had,
On their life as lived.

Good people,
Must suffer at times,
To experience living difficulties,
The less fortunate have known.

So they then know,
What needs to be done,
In order to help provide,
A better life for all.

Bad people for eternity,
Will suffer as well,
When the river to Hell's gate,
Is crossed over by them.

For they shall indeed,
Have all eternity,
To suffer, repent, wail, an cry,
For all misdeeds they did.

In Heaven is great joy,
Good is always known,
Never in Hell,
The bad shall see.

Children, innocents,
The old, lame, sick,
Helpeless ones all,
Those who suffered shall know.

That in God's Heaven,
All such suffering is replaced,
With love abundant, overflowing,
No suffering of anykind allowed.

Illness none,
Souls made perfect,
After life's travails,
All loved ones together again.

Eternity in God's care,
Promised by Jesus Christ,
For all to share,
Wonderful bliss for evermore.

No soul inflicted with pain,
Shall never be so again,
Trust abundant, safety assured,
Eternal love known by all.

Thank God then,
As life's problems unfold,
Because each soul grows on same,
For entry into heaven's eternity we know.

96

When

When life's burdens,
Seem ready to break,
One's very being apart.

A knee bent,
In heartfelt prayer,
Uttered from your soul comes forth.

Quietly sent,
To our Great Creator,
Our God of All.

Carried for you,
By one of His angels,
On wings of heavenly gold.

Placed in His,
Immediate in-box,
Already read by God.

A return reply,
Composed and delivered,
With lightening speed to you.

Fear not, despair not,
For your thoughts, and prayers,
Have already been heard.

Your life is not to be,
Crushed, spindled, mutilated,
Nor thrown away.

For no situation,
Is ever without fair solution,
No prayer ever overlooked.

Every act has,
A greater purpose,
Humanity's good shall prevail.

Just do your part,
Try your best, move forward,
Never quit, nor give up.

Remember the "I Am",
Your Creator and God,
Is always with you.

Remembering this,
Your burdens in life,
Are God's as well.

Always such burdens,
Have been assigned,
With care, a divine purpose in mind.

For your Creator and God,
Created same with purpose,
To aid your soul in eternity.

97

Love is Basic

Only love,
Can form a foundation,
For a life well lived.

Backed by action, work,
Good judgment, accomplishment,
Requiring the rock, called love.

For love of life, family, others,
Country as well,
Needs such an anchor in life.

Then the basics of life,
Created for all to share,
Are unshakeable for you.

Work found in innovation, creation,
Action, thoughts, insights, inspirations,
Come with love.

Always thinking, moving, acting on same,
Victories in life there will be,
Made with love.

In every effort,
Nothing should be wasted,
Time least of all, nor love.

With free will, freedoms for all,
Love too, let's show God,
What we can do!

98

Should, Could, Would

As I grow older,
Weighted down,
By many years.

A few simple words,
Ring over and over,
In my mind.

Over and over,
They sound, all three,
Like a tolling bell.

"Should, Could, Would",
Are the few,
Simple words.

Should rings first,
Loud, very loud,
Clear as a loud bell.

Questions it brings,
Actions done,
Wrong decisions made.

Perhaps meaning well,
Finished poorly,
Or not at all.

Should I have …..,
Should I have …..,
Should I have…...

Could is another tolling bell,
Of the three heard,
Ringing from years gone by.

Over and over,
Such a simple word,
Sounds loud in my mind.

What could have been,
Changed, altered,
Accomplished, done better.

Could I have….,
Could I have….,
Could I have…...,

Would rings its bell as well,
Throughout my many years,
Perhaps loudest of the three.

If I only would thought,
Have done more,
Corrected what I did.

What changes,
In my life's path,
Would have been seen.

Would I been….,
Would I saved….,
Would I bettered…..

I shall never know,
Life's true nswers,
To such simple words.

Now time is gone,
Years have passed,
Long passed me by.

Never to be lived,
Over again, never, in any way,
"Should, Could, Would" are now silent, as I pray.

99

Simple Moments

This morning,
As I started my day,
I heard a beautiful song,
An unknown bird began to sing.

True high notes,
Sweet, clear, inspiring,
Filling the air,
With glorious sound.

My spirit soared,
With its melody heard,
It seemed to proclaim,
How glorious living is.

As the sun appeared,
Rising in the morning sky,
The songbird's tune,
Rose in its beauty too.

What a blissful wonder,
Given by nature to me,
The bird's beautiful song,
Begining another day for me.

I asked myself,
Is it not wonderful,
Just being alive,
Hearing such entrance to my day.

Why are such simple things,
As a songbird's joy,
Sounded in its morning song,
Heard by all.

Bring more joy,
Lifing your very soul,
To wonderous hights,
More than treasures of gold?

Why is love,
Given by a spouse,
More valuable,
Than life itself?

No answers came,
To such questions asked,
As the beautiful song,
By the songbird ended.

The sun was up,
The day had begun,
The enchanted moment over,
Nature quite once more.

Alias,
Such simple moments,
Are lost in time,
But never forgotten, never, never, never....

100

My Twilight Years

Into each life lived,
On this earth of ours,
A assigned guardian angel,
Watches your years flow by.

Each grouping of years,
Has lessons to be learned,
Each has challenges,
Sometimes tears.

Toward our end years,
Called by many names,
But known by all,
As twilight years, I now enter.

Slower in walk,
Now for sure,
No longer able,
To run at all.

More joint pain,
Than ever before,
With sleep interrupted,
Throughout the night.

Carrying more weight,
Than needed for sure,
Now slower in walking,
Even sitting more often.

Napping, need says so,
My energies not full,
recharge often required,
That I certainly know.

Twilight of life beckons,
Now as I see me,
Slowly coming under,
Its carefully shaded tree.

I am worn in body, mind, spirit
Indeed much older too,
Now that my twilight is here,
I feel that my guardian angel is always near.

Rain

Falling from clouds above,
Rain cleansing, nurshing,
All life on this good earth.

Some say,
Its God's tears of joy,
Renewing life once more.

Gently may it fall upon us all,
Such a wonderful promise,
Given again, again, an again.

As such gentle rains fall,
Cleansing, purifying, renewing,
Washing us all.

Sometimes rain,
Comes in great gusts,
Blown by strong winds.

Brought in great storms,
Fiercer as fierce can be,
Darker than the darkest night.

Frightening they can be,
They pass above an around,
Perhaps a danger in the night.

But God's displeasure,
Crying such tears,
Lasts only moments in His sight.

However it comes,
Rains are always sought,
For life's sustaining needs.

So all such rain falling,
Upon your life's path,
May be gentle, I pray.

It's message is meant to be,
Slowly, gently, falling about,
Showing God's deep love for all.

Especially for you,
His approval grandly shown,
By giving you His gentle tears.

102

Mothers

Mothers give life,
To each human body,
God places the soul within.

Mothers provide love, safety,
A beginning for each child,
Long before birth.

Mothers give reassurance,
Stability, comfort, safety,
Guidance in each child's life.

Mothers are sought,
For valuable councel,
When life encounters occur.

Mothers provide to each,
Love, reassurance, advice,
We learn about living from them.

Mothers are supporting,
Encouraging, forgiving,
Giving unmeasureable love.

Mothers were made,
To renew life on this earth,
Protecting same in ever way.

Mothers are indeed,
A fountain of love, comfort,
Giving us their all.

So we thank our God,
His enduring gift of love,
For our mothers.

Unexpected Rain

When unexpected rain,
Falls upon you,
On your path of life.

Always gentle,
Watering your way,
May it be.

Washing away,
All your troubles,
Very carefully.

When sunshine comes,
Once again upon you,
May it gently dry troubles away.

Knowing once again,
Everything is made right,
Right as it can be once more.

And may God's angels,
Continue watching, caring, protecting,
Helping you with life's unexpected rains.

104

Another Day Begins

I watch in early morning,
The first rays of heaven's sun,
Wakening another day.

Quietly, they come,
So very, very quietly,
Not even a babe stirs.

Nor flower petals move, all is still,
All not yet aware, all silent,
As early dawn begins, once more.

No response by any,
As ray by ray,
Very, very quietly, comes a new day.

But a day begins,
As another, then another,
Rays of sun, join together.

For life itself must stir,
Once more for another day,
Say the great orb's rays.

Even peaks of mountains,
High above us all,
Cannot stop another day.

Waking all, ray by ray,
But not with cries,
Just quietly, very quietly.

Soon all of the earth,
Is fully aware,
Another day is arriving.

To be used,
Joyfully, carefully, wondrously,
Lived by all.

Another gift,
From the Most High,
Another day, another day, another day.

For all to do,
With what they will,
A treasured gift of time bestowed, another day.

Priceless,
Rare,
With none to spare, another day.

For all life now is astir,
Never bothering to count,
How many rays it takes, another day.

Nor how much silence,
Each ray may break,
As each shines down, another day.

For another day,
A treasured gift,
Bestowing life once more, another day.

By our Creator who walks,
Quietly, very silently,
Like His rising sun's rays, another blessed day.

105

Life's Seasons

Your soul is created,
By God Himself,
Implated into your forming body,
Within your mother.

Then a major miracle,
Occurs once more in time,
You burst down the birth channel,
Beginning your life's first season.

Your Spring begins,
Full of life, loved, growing, playing,
Unfolding many mysteries,
Crawling, walking, talking, dreaming.

Worries, responsibilities, cares, troubles,
Are not yours at all,
Just sleep, grow, progress each day,
Providing love and great joy for all.

Learning at every moment,
Developing senses to the fullest,
Crawling, walking, talking,
Learning quickly all.

Soon childhood is achieved,
Playing with others,
Social skills learned,
Time rushes you onward.

Physical skills develop,
Emotions emerge,
Personality develops,
Its You for sure.

Alas, Spring is over,
Early Summer arrives,
Formal schooling begins,
Kindergarten, school starts.

School is a vast learning of facts,
Forcing mental abilities to the max,
But its a kind season,
Total growth beyond measure.

Mid-Summer soon begins,
You enter years know as "teens",
Joyful times abound,
For teen years bounce around.

Now a condition called "maturity" sought,
Rarely found, cannot be taught,
So the quest now starts,
For body, mind, and soul to mature.

Expansion into young adulthood begins,
Temptations to fail are many,
In one manner or another,
We all do, but its still you.

Mid-Summer teaches you to overcome,
Failures, great, small, character is built,
Strength comes from struggles,
Its great teacher is called "failure".

Your growth continues,
As late summer begins,
High School demands growth,
Offering many skills to learn.

Late summer continues,
Into your early twenty years,
College, military service, work starts,
All in late summer's shinning sphere.

With great luck in the other sex,
God introduces to you a mate,
Enchanting, perfect, in all aspects,
Carrying a lifetime's love, just for you.

Summer is over, early Fall arrives,
Marriage, children, responsibilities galore,
Real lessons in life begin,
Work, needs of family, obligations to met.

Never enough time, or funds,
Life's full enjoyment is yours,
Love abundant, growth, success,
Challenges met, life is for you.

Mid-Fall arrives, life's cup overflows,
Family, love, warm glorious emotions,
The taste of life's full measured savored,
How good life can be.

Maturity occurs within, without, an about,
Goals complete, happiness is yours,
Late-Fall is entered, now completed,
Your soul shouts out the final season is here.

Its early winter, your" Golden Days" now start,
Announced by slower step, added caution,
With new sensed aches never felt before,
A milestone called retirement, just for you.

Midwinter arrives so soon after,
Like a thief at night, not invited,
It cannot be stopped, as time progresses,
Each season must be lived.

Late winter comes to soon,
Memories shared, family, love, final maturity,
Eternity yet to start, your soul to return,
Whenever God requires it back.

Challenges overcome, work accomplished,
Because of your efforts, love, and sacrifices,
Helping all, caring, loving ever moment,
Life itself seemed now complete.

Late-winter allows more joys of life's wonders,
Music, remembrances, love, of caring souls,
Whose life's paths crossed yours,
The full poetry of living it all.

Remembering loved ones, experiences,
Freedoms found, literature's read,
The eternal soul now clearly sees,
Of one's departed married mate so dear.

Now Late-Winter time allows needed wisdom,
Backward and forward on time's final line,
Soon God will send His souls harvester,
Called by many names, but fear not.

For God does so,
With grace, redemption, His love of all,
Remembering Jesus Christ's promise of old,
Your place assured in His heavenly abode.

An eternity with all loved ones,
All cares banished, immeasurable love about,
Your soul mate will meet you at heaven's gate,
In an eternity assured, by God's promise to you!

106

Dreams on Life's Path

Every dream you have,
Is stored away,
Never lost,
Not at all.

Perhaps remembered,
Perhaps not,
Because life moves forward,
But dreams are still within.

Dreams start early,
Before your journey,
As you slumber,
In your mother's womb.

Suddenly your slumbers,
Are ended as your soul,
Inserted by God Himself,
Creates the full you.

Now as a babe,
Your dreams are yours,
Yours alone,
For evermore.

Following your path,
Founded by parents genes,
Abilities glore,
Life has imbedded in you.

Childhood dreams,
Such as being cowboy, Indian Chief,
Other hero images too,
Are in your dreams.

In older youth,
Dreams come more often,
More realistic,
Often from actual experiences.

Some forgotten,
Some remembered,
More mature dreams,
Filtering life for you.

Then as you mature,
Dreams may turn into goals,
Hopefully to be achieved,
For they are real to you.

Failures may occur,
But successes do to,
Dreams shaping life,
Into reality itself.

In full maturity of years,
Some dreams fulfilled,
Many not, but so what,
Dreams are only dreams.

However your life is shaped,
By circumstance or choice,
Even by unseen other ways,
Dreams are not forgotten.

May you wish upon a star,
All far, far, far away,
Hoping a dream unfulfilled,
Can still come true.

Fully knowing,
It is but a wish,
A hope, a distant desire,
Never ever to be.

Finally life closes in,
For all living things,
No exceptions allowed,
Including you.

Dreams can be recalled,
Making your life lived,
More abundant in love,
ind acts, good deeds done.

All remembered,
Perhaps as dreams,
Perhaps real,
Can be taken with you.

Into God's heaven,
Through heaven's gate,
With Saint Peter's blessing
To share in eternity.

Heaven is not a dream,
But a sure promise,
From Jesus Christ,
God Himself in another form.

That your eternal final dream,
Is true as sunlight, earth,
Water, and air,
You live in today.

Your past loved ones,
Already there,
Await with eternal joy,
Your appointed time to arrive.

So your final dream,
Is not lost, misplaced,
Or every failed you,
An eternity with loved ones, is true.

A Daughter's Valentine

From the time,
I first saw you,
My wonderful daughter,
My heart glowed.

Indeed,
My heart beat with pride,
Because God gave me,
Such a perfect gift, you.

A special life,
Provide by your mother,
With God above,
Supplying your untainted soul.

Perfection, beauty, life,
Provided again to me,
Just once more,
Placed under my protective care.

Over the years,
Your mother and I,
Watched with pride,
Your meeting many challenges.

All conquered I say,
With grace, charm, thought,
Or common sense,
All in ample supply.

As you met life,
On all its varied fields,
You were challenged,
But a winner every time.

No circumstances,
Unexpected, unforeseen,
Nor any setback,
Ever defeated you.

Always marching forward,
On your chosen life's path,
Positive, confident,
Displaying great assurance.

Forward you moved,
Adding experiences, learning,
Making gains,
Growing, maturing.

Now you are mature,
A great teacher of the young,
Forming future lifes to be lived,
Molding their life's to come.

Shaping futures of society,
Yet to unfold,
Building better lifes
In the future to see.

My daughter,
Small as you were,
Now a giant,
In accomplishments, spirit too.

Your mother and I,
Surly God as well,
Are so very pleased,
That our love created you.

Indeed, we firmily believe,
Family, friends, students,
Former or present,
Will love you always too.

So daughter, we are pleased,
Very pleased, to ask you,
Please be our special Valentine,
On this Saint Valentine's Day!

My Plea as I Grow Older

Remember my promise dear,
If I lived to grow old,
I shall still need you forever,
That I know.

Your spirit, charm, beauty,
Your very love of life,
Family, friends, people,
Are still with me.

My memory of you,
Has never faded, dimmned,
Been misplaced, nor forgotton,
In any way, my love.

Not of you,
My sweet one,
As it is imbedded,
Deep, so very deep, in my heart.

Always remembered,
Never forgotten,
No matter as years pass,
Or what else occurs.

The very world about me,
Can cease to be,
But not my memories,
Of all our years together.

Our life and years together,
Will always be remembered,
As a love never ever,
To be forgotten.

Never of you,
My dearest one,
Never lost or misplaced,
For even one brief moment.

Your smile, voice, touch, love,
All dearly remembered,
All freely given,
All vital to my life with you.

Your presence lost,
Your untimely death,
Leaving me empty,
My very soul still hurting so.
My great lady's wondrous spirit,
Personified in grace, charm,
Quiet fimminity, radiating love,
Such inner beauty admired by all.

All comprising you,
Only you, no one else,
Given to me,
In such a wondrous way.

Now you have left me,
Called to God's heavenly kingdom,
Earlier than I ever thought,
Needed there before me.

Granted your eternal rest,
From all of your ills,
Life's trials, troubles,
Suffering in your last years.

To spend in God's eternity,
With your loved ones,
Needing you there,
Called to your eternal home.

Yet I know that you will,
Wait for me in heaven,
As you have, and will,
Remembering this plea of mine.

So my love,
My time now grows shorter,
Here day by the day,
To stay here, that I know.

Yet I have more to do,
Before I come to you,
Sharing eternity together,
For ever more.

Apparently God Himself,
Has a bit more for me to do,
So stand by in eternity,
At its gates for now.

Just remember me as I grow older,
God will call me home too,
I shall be with you, once again,
Together, my love, for all eternity.

109

What Words Can Do

Take care with words,
Spoken, written,
Remembered,
Used without care.

Remember such words,
Perhaps cause great pain,
Harm, consequences, to come,
That one must bare.

Once spoken,
Uttered in haste, or anger,
Without thought,
May never be forgotten.

Only remembered,
Embedded in memories,
Not to be abandoned,
Nor forever lost, just remembered.

Words can praise,
Express hope, love,
Success, achievements,
Glorious feelings needed by all.

Words can convey brilliant ideas,
Tremendous knowledge,
Encouraging living right,
Giveing life wonderful meaning.

Raising individuals,
Families, nations,
To achieve with wonderous effort,
Dreamed of goals.

Words can express, convey,
Beautiful human emotions,
Love, kindness, graitude, mercy,
All so needed in life.

Indeed, words,
Are very powerful,
Spoken or written,
Conveying thoughts to others.

Traversing time itself,
When written down,
Clearly, concisely, meaning carried,
Read by those yet to be.

Unknown future generations,
May read, understand,
Ignore, accept, reject,
Ideas expressed by written words.

Clearly, words travel,
Through time itself,
Well beyond the time,
Of who wrote them down.

Knowledge, information,
instructions, descriptions,
Hard won over generations,
Transfered by words into the future.

Beauty, philosophy,
Religion, history,
Science, engineering,
All are conveyed.

Words in this present,
So very important now,
Expand human thoughts,
Passed on to future generations.

Remember,
Just how powerful,
Words really are,
From the past, present, into the future.

What words do, can do,
Or should not do,
Can not be known fully,
Please use your words with care!

Christmas in Moscow

T'was the night,
Before Christmas,
And all through her apartment,
Nothing was stirring.

Not even a Lisa,
She was fast asleep,
Dreaming of sugar plums,
Pudding, and Russian borsch.

It was a Russian winter,
Well below freezing,
Outside, snow, ice, wind,
Very cold, frozen, dangerous.

Still her dreams,
Were warm, cozy,
Toasty, comfortable,
As a fireplace fire.

Keeping her warm,
Deep in her slumber,
In her dreamland,
A world restful and bliss.

Suddenly, noise,
In the middle of a snowy,
Frozen Moscow winter night,
Disturbing her sleep.

A loud knocking,
At her door,
Knock, knock, knock,
Was waking her up.

A loud voice demanded in,
For a hot vodka tonic,
Along with smaller voices,
Saying the same.

Lisa put her house robe,
About her chilled body,
Slipped on her Russian bear skin house shoes,
Then stomped to the door.

Then she was demanding,
Who, why, what,
Was knocking,
Knock, knocking at her door.

An answer came,
Very loud and clear,
It is I, Father Christmas,
And my elf helpers.

Come to bring presents,
To a lost Texas great lady,
As well as some Texas cheer,
On this Christmas eve's night.

After all, you deserve,
A great big "Howdy Y'All",
Brought from Texas by us,
Directly to you.

From all family, friends,
Others in Texas that love you so,
On this Christmas Day,
All send a "Texas Merry Christmas" to you!!

Slaves to Credit

Least we forget,
The credit master says,
Ours is to work,
Not to rest.

Ours is to struggle,
To pull,
To push,
To strain.

Ours is to serve,
To grovel,
To bend,
To tow.

We are not to think,
Dream,
Hope,
A wish upon a star only is ours.

Least we forget,
Ours is to submit,
Not to question,
The credit master's whip is quick.

Even deadly at times, as the asp,
We must not forget,
The credit master's ego,
To feed and pamper it.

Never offend, truth hidden,
The tongue silent,
Salvation is fleeting,
Like moonlight on desert sands.

Least, we forget,
Ours is to endure,
Yet not cry out,
Ours is to just dream.

Of achieving joy,
Perhaps paradise too,
Not as credit slaves,
But to be free.

For now ours is to beg,
Plead, seek mercy,
Never demand,
For nothing is ours.

Only the illusion exists,
As our life slowly ebbs away,
Until the debt is payed,
The credit master is in charge!!

112

Ode to Credit Slaves

At best pain will go,
Bad will vanish,
Paradise will be ours,
Slaves make the world move.

Master's make the slave toil,
Hang head low,
Advert the eyes,
Dare not speak the truth.

Make the slave toil,
Move, tote, work,
Ask not from the Maser,
He makse the slave toil.

Waste not,
Worry,
Hurry,
Make the slave toil.

Never stand tall,
Always bend, carry,
Be wary,
Make the slave toil.

Think not,
Reason be gone,
Master's way a must,
Make the slave toil.

Slave toil,
Slave toil,
Slave toil,
Slave toil.

Kedp the credit flowing,
Keep the loans comming,
Keep the slave eager,
Keep the slave dreaming.

Toiler is the slave,
The master reaps,
The slave weeps,
Make the slave toil!!

Spring Breezes

Spring breezes,
Floating softly by,
Like butterflies,
Quitely flying by.

In the still part,
Of the evening,
Very welcomed,
So softly felt.

Bringing a scent,
Loved by all,
Provideing an aroma,
Of life anew.

As senses,
Once thought dead,
Spring to life once more,
For just one brief moment.

Perhaps a golden, beautiful,
Full moon is present too,
Floating so high above,
Crossing the eternal sky.

A sky filled with multitudes,
Of uncountable stars,
Shining down radiance,
Begun from long ago.

Even our sister planets,
Seem to stop spinning,
For a moment, just briefly,
In a small bit of time.

Because spring breezes,
Reminds one of long past thoughts,
Wonderful loving memories,
So meaningful, never ever to be forgotten.

114

To Live Forever Here?

I have thought,
What it would be like,
To live forever,
On this earth.

After much thought,
Dear God,
Your divine limit,
On every life is best.

Why, one asks,
I have an answer,
To offer unto all,
It follows now below.

Such answer might seem,
Shallow, limited, weak,
Unreasoned, even faulty,
To others perhaps.

Time is limited,
For any human life,
On this earthly sphere,
Because God made it so.

However in deep thought,
Great reasoning applied,
Continuing life's struggles,
Forever here is not living.

But instead,
It would be a sentence,
To everlasting torment,
Of body and soul on earth.

As such,
Any human would experience,
Terrible unbearable suffering,
Far beyond our capacities.

Each would see,
Current loved ones live, die,
While his life continued,
Ever onward on a endless path.

As each valued loved one,
assed away, soul freed,
Witnessed by the timeless one,
Sorrow, grief, would boundlessly build.

In his sorrow,
Helplessness to intervene,
Death itself claims of his,
Each valued loved one.

Such would bring the timeless one,
Un-surmountable pain,
o his body, mind, emotions,
Even to his eternal soul.

Life itself,
Forever on this earth,
Would then become,
An unbearable burden endured.

He would pray,
Beg entry,
Through Heaven's gate,
Joining all loved in so many times.

His many loved ones,
In his life's times lived,
Certainly already present,
Waiting, waiting, waiting, for him.

When his Book of Many Lifes,
Large it surely must be,
Is found, opened, read,
story of sorrow will unfold.

Struggling over an over,
In each life lived,
Encountering problems,
Much the same again, an again.

However, finally now in Heaven,
His soul is saved,
All will be forgiven,
By God Himself.

About this Book

This book was written to give the reader an introductory look at not only Texas, but many of its values that the majority of Texans themselves hold so dear.

Among which is a strong belief in our Creator, living in a free democratic society, individual liberties based on our written national and state constitutions, the rule of commonsense law, the worth of family, the value of friends, and one's individuals efforts.

It certainly was not meant even to come close to the great poets found throughout history in every country, around this wonderful, beautiful planet, which God provided to each of us for living our individual life

Such poets as Homer (epic poems), Chaucer (old English poetry), Pope (satirical poems), Omar Okayama (the Rubaiyat), Dickinson (True rhyme) or Carl isle (religious poetry), King David (Psalms) and so many more are found throughout many countries in every age.

They are another view of insight into the wonder of just being alive, full of emotions, illustrating the glorious taste of life's challenges, which God provides each of us.

This old Texan hopes that the serious reader has enjoyed the thoughts, emotions, and observations made in each of his poems.

They are not meant to be on the level of the great poets but still hoped to be thoughtful by conveying its meaning to each reader.

Just remember, poetry can be one of God's greatest gifts to you, just as His love for you is.

May you have a healthy, full, meaningful life filled with love for for all and look forward always.

> The Old Texan
> Granbury, Texas

About the Author

Roy Buford Jackson was born, raised, and educated in the capitol city of, Austin, Texas.

Roy received his bachelor's degree from The University of Texas in Austin and his masters degree from The University of Texas in Arlington.

He had a long career in engineering with major companies (35 years), followed by becoming a system/software contractor (20 years).

Roy was well known for producing logical focused solutions to major efforts in commercial and military projects. This included communications, aircraft, weapons, defense systems, and in other project areas as well.

Roy's s marriage (53 years) developed in him a deep spiritual, poetic view, with eternal love for his wonderful talented wife (Laura Jo Holley Jackson, now in God's hands), and the family she produced for him (Roy James, Lisa, Mark, and Luke).

Roy Buford Jackson, "An Old Texan", currently lives in Granbury, Texas.